W9-ABG-370

Language Rights in
French Canada

Francophone Cultures and Literatures

Tamara Alvarez-Detrell and Michael G. Paulson
General Editors

Vol. 2

PETER LANG
New York • Washington, D.C./Baltimore • San Francisco
Bern • Frankfurt am Main • Berlin • Vienna • Paris

Pierre A. Coulombe

Language Rights in French Canada

PETER LANG
New York • Washington, D.C./Baltimore • San Francisco
Bern • Frankfurt am Main • Berlin • Vienna • Paris

Library of Congress Cataloging-in-Publication Data

Coulombe, Pierre, A.
   Language rights in French Canada / Pierre A. Coulombe.
      p. cm. — (Francophone cultures and literatures; vol. 2)
   Includes bibliographical references and index.
   1. Language policy—Canada. 2. Civil rights—Canada. 3. French-
Canadians—Ethnic identity. I. Title. II. Series.
P119.32.C3C68   306.4'4971—dc20   94-11415
ISBN 0-8204-2504-4
ISSN 1077-0186

Die Deutsche Bibliothek-CIP-Einheitsaufnahme

Coulombe, Pierre A.:
Language rights in French Canada / Pierre A. Coulombe. - New York;
Washington D.C./Baltimore; San Francisco; Bern; Frankfurt am Main;
Berlin; Vienna; Paris: Lang.
   (Francophone cultures and literatures; Vol. 2)
   ISBN 0-8204-2504-4
NE: GT

Cover design by Nona Reuter.

The paper in this book meets the guidelines for permanence and durability
of the Committee on Production Guidelines for Book Longevity of the
Council of Library Resources.

Printed in the United States of America.

Contents

Preface

First a few words about the context in which this book was written. In recent years there has been much constitutional and political uncertainty over French Canada's place in the federation. Two historical attempts at amending the Canadian Constitution, the Meech Lake Accord and the Charlottetown Agreement, failed. The separatist Parti Québécois is in power once again in Québec, and plans (once again) to hold a referendum on independence before the end of 1995. At the federal level, the separatist Bloc Québécois and the Reform Party (notorious for its positions against French Canada and official bilingualism) have both made a formidable ascension to a more than ever polarized Parliament. Another group whose raison-d'être is to oppose official bilingualism, the Confederation of Regions Party (CoR), forms the opposition in New Brunswick's legislature.

The main themes of this book were developed around the time the Meech Lake Accord was being defeated by its adversaries. I was not so much surprised to hear Canadians oppose a special status for Québec than I was to hear them invoke the risks that such a status would pose to human rights. In due course the Charlottetown Agreement, too, would be rejected on similar grounds. Meanwhile, those who continue to oppose official bilingualism increasingly invoke individual rights in their protest. It seems as if most of French Canada's claims are somehow being condemned as an affront to justice.

There are reasons for worrying about this state of affairs. As a Québec-born French Canadian who grew up in Ontario and now lives in New Brunswick, I worry about the ideological assault against the language rights of French Canadians and Acadians. That there are people who object to such rights is of course not new. What is new is how the various charges against French Canada are increasingly inspired by a certain kind of liberal discourse which endows them with a powerful legitimacy. I also worry because French Canada is itself infused with this liberal discourse, and becomes ill-equipped to justify its language policies without appearing inconsistent. All sides proclaiming the modernity of their respective projects, the debate naturally ends up in the wrong arena featuring Québec versus Ottawa. It is not surprising, then, that some Québec separatists should sell independence as a panacea.

Since this book is partly based on a doctoral dissertation that was defended in June 1992 at the University of Western Ontario, I would like to acknowledge the invaluable help of my thesis supervisor, Richard Vernon, who generously shared many of his ideas and much of his time. I also wish to thank Douglas Long and Martin Westmacott at the University of Western Ontario, and Guy Laforest at the Université Laval, for their encouragements. While writing the thesis, I received financial support from the Government of Ontario and from the University of Western Ontario's Faculty of Graduate Studies and Department of Political Science.

As far as the preparation of the book goes, I am indebted to Diane Roussel who provided helpful comments on various drafts, and who discussed at length these issues with me. A note of appreciation goes to Claire Ryan for reading Part I of the manuscript and improving it in both form and content. I also wish to thank Karim Ismaili, with whom I had several conversations on the subject. I owe much to Heidi Burns at Peter Lang Publishing, not only for her technical assistance, but for her flexibility and support as well. Nona Reuter, also at Lang, was very helpful in the final stage of production. Finally, I am grateful to my students at the University of Western Ontario and at the University of New Brunswick who helped me clarify my thoughts during various seminar discussions on French Canada.

Introduction

Some people look upon language conflicts with cynicism, if not indifference, as if these were yet another episode of the great Canadian drama. Perhaps they feel that Canadian politics is saturated with the issue of French Canada, source of tiresome debates and periodic constitutional overloads. After all, French-English relations have often occupied centre-stage throughout our history, admittedly sometimes to the detriment of other pressing issues. Westerners have long charged that their grievances were not being heard given Ottawa's apparent rush to accommodate French Canadians, who today only number a few in their part of the country. It may even have become politically incorrect to discuss French Canada in an age when questions relating to jobs, Aboriginals, and the environment, to name a few, seem more urgent. The debate over French Canada, it is said, has diverted our attention and energies away from the real problems. Such is at least the sentiment often expressed in the media, universities, and public hearings on constitutional reform.

Yet some of our deepest political values and convictions are periodically put to the test when language conflicts find their way up to the national agenda. It has certainly been the case during the last thirty years when debates over official bilingualism and Québec's language laws more than once forced Canadians into self-examination. During that period, linguistic conflicts have become more acute with increased state language planning at both federal and provincial levels of government.

Looking back at these debates, one has the sense that everything has been said and that our failures are, at the end of the day, the result of our own inability to come to terms with the French-English duality. Recent constitutional reforms, from the 1982 Constitution Act to the defunct Charlottetown Agreement, sadly displayed this inability. Still, despite our constitutional fatigue, we should not neglect the implications of having persistent conceptual ambiguities about those political values and convictions that underlie language issues. Canada's very existence hinges on our capacity to manage the tensions that inevitably arise in a multinational state and to understand each other's discourses and appreciate the different values that are at stake.

French Canada has anything but become irrelevant. Its relevance, however, goes beyond the importance we place on the constitutional future of the Canadian federation. More significant is how the question of French Canada tells us something about community in a liberal society. Many of the problems we face, it would seem, are not so much rooted in federalism as they are in liberal society itself.

While there is a consensus that certain kinds of language rights have firm foundations in a liberal society like Canada, stronger or far-reaching language rights face far more obstacles. Many of these obstacles are surely cultural, such as the views that some anglophones still have on the English language itself. They believe that the dominance of English over French is the product of social Darwinism, that some languages are naturally destined to eclipse others because they are better adapted. They perceive English as the pragmatic language of modernity and scientific objectivity which have supposedly rid themselves of particular cultural and ethnic content. English, in other words, is a neutral, universal language not specific to any culture in particular. The state should therefore also be neutral and not interfere with the natural selection of languages and cultures. French, on the other hand, is perceived as the language of refinement and flamboyancy, perhaps well suited for the salons of high society and for enhancing romantic encounters, but of no use in the hard world of business. As for those who find some remedial cultural value in French, they (in any case) often believe that the French spoken in Canada has little to do with "real" French—the kind they associate with "Parisian" French. It is no wonder that those who hold those beliefs object to language rights for French Canadians and Acadians, for they do not find much practical worth to the French language to begin with. [1]

The main obstacles, however, are ideological, such as denouncing the alleged preferential treatment of French-Canadian minorities outside Québec and the resulting injustice for other ethnic minorities. This view unfortunately finds support among Canadians, especially when it is wrapped in the appropriate political discourse. After all, how could we not desire a united Canada where all citizens are treated equally, whatever their origins? Official bilingualism, in that respect, becomes nothing more than preferential treatment for one group resulting in unfair treatment of other linguistic minorities who do not have this "privilege".

Or again, it is often said that Québec's language legislation, notably Bill 101, is the ultimate expression of unequal treatment since it deliberately favors the majority culture in the province at the expense of all others, including the anglophone minority. Discriminatory practices and limits to freedom of expression is how the Québec state promotes a particular community: the French-Canadian community. Bill 101, it is widely believed, is nothing but a plain violation of basic individual rights, all in the name of Québec's alleged community rights.

The Acadians of New Brunswick must also face similar obstacles. For example, some opponents to the constitutional entrenchment of Bill 88, which guarantees Acadian and English *communities* certain rights, have charged that it undermines our liberal system of individual rights. They claim that the amendment amounts to a recognition of collective rights, hence to an unacceptable transfer of power from the individual to the community. Such a precedent, they argue, does not sit well with our views about what rights are meant to achieve in the first place and, in that sense, runs counter to liberal principles.

Whether we are talking about official bilingualism at the federal level, Québec's Bill 101, or New Brunswick's Bill 88, these are all being challenged by a liberal discourse which relies on a partial view of the Charter. Attempts at regulating language use by way of constitutional or legislative dispositions are being treated as unreasonable restrictions on fundamental rights.

Canada's liberal political culture indeed draws heavily on the Charter of Rights and Freedoms, which since 1982 entrenches in the Canadian Constitution the kinds of rights that are most valued in liberal democracies: fundamental freedoms, such as the freedoms of religion, expression, and association; democratic rights, such as the right to vote; mobility rights to live anywhere in the country, and to leave it if desired; legal rights that pertain to the criminal process, such as the rights to a trial and to be presumed innocent until proven guilty; rights against discrimination on the basis of sex, ethnic origin, and age. We value these rights because they are the concrete expression of our belief in the dignity and autonomy of the individual.

But the Charter also recognizes special rights to some Canadians in virtue of their belonging in a particular community. Francophones outside Québec and anglophones within Québec have the right to receive education and federal government services in their language where the numbers warrant. There is a reference to the province of New Brunswick, where official bilingualism and the equality of Acadian and English communities are guaranteed. The Charter also instructs judges to consider Canada's multicultural heritage when relevant. Moreover, the rights and privileges of Aboriginal peoples receive an explicit safeguard against the subordination of their own rights to those of the Charter. All of these community rights are unrelated to the rights that are owed to us as members of a liberal polity, and have everything to do with duties we acquired throughout the history and circumstances of a country permeated by the French-English duality, its multicultural character, and its indigenous communities.

Furthermore, a central feature of the Charter is how it leaves room for compromise and balance when individual interests clash with social goals that are judged to be worthy. The very first section states that all Charter rights are subject to reasonable limits if the Courts rule that their exercise undermines important legislative objectives. There is also a controversial section, the "notwithstanding" clause, that gives any government the power to override specific Charter rights with a simple legislation, regardless of judicial decisions. If the notwithstanding clause seems to defeat the purpose of having rights in the first place, in Canada it is felt that parliamentary supremacy must not be weakened too much by the increased role of the judiciary.

All in all, the Charter is a constitutional document which attempts to protect the individual rights that are widely recognized in liberal societies, to enshrine a deep-rooted tradition of accommodation between French and English communities, and to allow the pursuit of social goals that must sometimes take precedence over the individual's solitary interests. In other words, the Charter is not a purely individualistic document since it recognizes community rights and goals.

The deeper impact of the Charter has been to transform Canada's political culture by reinforcing citizens' allegiance to the Canadian nation and weakening provincial attachments. [2] The Charter was meant to be a nation-building tool, one that would run counter to the federal nature of the country. Charter rights would have a universalizing effect since Canadians would be guaranteed equal rights coast to coast, over and above local preferences and needs. But the Charter would not simply stand apart as a constitutional document, for it would merge with our sense of nationhood, become constitutive of our sense of community. Allegiance would be displaced from the province to the nation, power from legislatures to the courts.

The Charter had not been in place ten years that political culture in English-speaking Canada had already evolved along those lines. But more importantly, this emerging political culture also began to see the Charter as the symbol of a triumphant liberal individualism, a sign that Canada had become a true modern country. Advocates of community rights would soon be charged with an offence against the Charter in particular and against liberalism in general. In that sense, the new individualism turned its back on a long tradition of collectivism in Canada. As early as 1774, the British recognized the community rights of the colony of Québec. The first constitution of modern Canada itself, the British North America Act of 1867 (B. N. A. Act), reflected a philosophy where communities would have their place: special rights were granted to Protestant and Catholic minorities, not to mention the federal division of powers which would give Québec partial control over its own affairs.

But however foreign the idea of a symmetrical equality between citizens and the sanctity of their individual rights is to Canada's collectivist tradition, it has taken over public consciousness in the post-Charter era. What were once considered special rights rooted in the history of French-English duality are now treated as unacceptable privileges for French Canada. Minority language rights themselves, the Charter's centre-piece, are seen as an aberration within the logic of uniform equality, to be shed along with all the vestiges of special treatment that pose an obstacle to Canada's liberal culture. Official bilingualism, entrenched in the Charter, is now paradoxically being challenged by the Charter culture itself. Needless to say, Québec's own language legislation is more than ever becoming an object of scorn for its restrictions on individual rights. In the eyes of many English-speaking Canadians, then, the Charter not only is a nation-building tool but also a document that celebrates liberal individualism.

By undermining Canada's federal structure and collective values, the Charter culture constitutes a double assault against French Canada. The belief that community rights have no validity in liberal society is grafted on the belief that federalism is an obstacle to Canadian nationhood. Every Canadian is owed the same rights as a member of the Canadian nation, regardless of provincial or regional belonging, and every individual is owed the same rights as a member of a liberal society, regardless of community belonging. Thus the traditional critique against French Canada, whether it be against Québec's claim to special status or against official bilingualism, is reaching new heights with a powerful discourse based on liberal justice. In that sense, French Canada is not threatened so much by its lack of status within the federation, but rather by a liberal ideology that is increasingly unsympathetic to state language planning.

This book is, above all, a defence of language rights in French Canada. But it reaches beyond arguments for language rights since they cut across a deeper problem. The problem I am concerned with is the place of community in liberal society, which today often takes the form of a conflict between individual rights and collective rights. The possibility of there being a coherent and justifiable conception of community rights, one which might in turn apply to language rights in French Canada, must therefore be examined.

The presentation is in two parts. Part I focuses on the question of community in liberalism and is largely inspired by the Anglo-American debate between liberals and communitarians. The discussion in this first part addresses theoretical issues that are not confined to the Canadian experience and that could therefore easily apply to other societies. My aim in chapter 1 is to define two different kinds of belonging, one in the liberal community, and the other in the community of identity. To this end, I describe the core values of liberalism, including the value of individual rights, and I outline the meaning of communal goods and identity. Chapter 2 tackles the problem more directly by examining whether the logic of liberal society poses a problem for the promotion of communal goods, and whether it can even undermine a community's attempts to survive. I address the tension between the liberal requirement of maximizing personal autonomy, and the preservation of the cultural context in which communal goods are nurtured. In chapter 3, I ask if community rights make any sense, and if they are a justifiable counterweight to individualistic rights-discourse. The objective is to sort out which versions of community rights are plausible, and which ones ought to be discarded. Chapter 4 serves as a transition to part II by introducing the question of language. I explore what sociolinguists tell us about some of the real and supposed links between language and identity.

Part II applies these questions to Canada, more specifically to Québec and New Brunswick. Chapter 5 is historical in perspective, as it traces the role of the French language in defining the respective identities of French Canadians and Acadians. In chapter 6, I discuss the justifications for state language planning in a market-oriented society. I also discuss the claim that far-reaching language planning is not only necessary to French Canadians and Acadians, but that it is owed to them. Chapter 7 examines the evolution of language policy in Québec, from the first modest attempts at legislating the use of French to the more substantial (and controversial) Bill 101. The objective is to evaluate the legitimacy of Québec's language policy in the light of various court rulings. Chapter 8 examines the notion of citizenship, a notion that is central to our understanding of language rights in Canada. The discussion brings to the forefront New Brunswick's public conception of French-English relations in the context of Bill 88.

A note on the book's title. I realize it may irritate some Québécois readers who believe that French Canada is somewhat of an antiquated concept, or who feel that it negates the existence of Québec as a full-fledged political community. But my choice reflects a desire to include all those people who share this common language and origin, whether they live in Acadia, Québec, Ontario, or anywhere else. French Canada is a community whose only boundaries are the French-Canadian and Acadian personalities themselves. No semantic substitution or redesigning of the map, past or future, could change this.

Notes

1.   On these perceptions, see Report of the task force on official languages,
      Towards Equality of the Official Languages in New Brunswick (March 1982),
      62-70.

2.   About the impact of the Charter on Canada's political culture, see Alan C.
      Cairns' various articles in *Disruptions: Constitutional Struggles, from the
      Charter to Meech Lake*, ed. Douglas E. Williams (Toronto: McClelland and
      Stewart, 1991).

Part I

Community in Liberalism

1

Competing Communities

Liberalism is the ideological background against which we can conceive conflicts over language rights in Canada. As we saw, it is an important ingredient to the political culture that has grown out of the Canadian Charter of Rights and Freedoms. Though not always explicitly, those who oppose far-reaching language rights often rely on liberal discourse in making their case, arguing, for example, that such a law is illiberal because it restricts individual rights. It therefore becomes important to understand what liberalism is all about, or at least which of its core values are involved in the language debate. The liberal community in Canada—for liberalism is, after all, the foundation of a community—is challenged by our need for deep attachments that say something about who we are, or who we think we are. It is, in other words, confronted with a competing community whose worth rests on the communal goods it fosters. The hard question, as we shall see in Part II, is whether French Canada can reach a balance amongst the competing values that each community offers to realize. We must first consider what these values are all about.

What does it mean to be liberal? For one thing, liberalism distinguishes itself from other ideologies in the way it separates issues of morality from the organization of political society. Given a plurality of opposing and sometimes incommensurable views of the world, liberals believe that no single philosophy of life should be imposed on citizens by the state or should dominate over the basic institutions of society. In that sense, liberalism is essentially *political*, not metaphysical, as John Rawls puts it; that is, the liberal conception of justice is independent of controversial philosophical doctrines about human nature. [1] Richard Vernon further suggests that liberalism is not about philosophical discourse, whose validity comes from resolving differences by one moral proposition winning over others, but about a conception of politics where "the fact of individual distinctness [is] given constitutional weight; in which individuals or their interests are not subsumed under others', in which each pursues interests or follows reasons or makes choices which are 'his own'".[2] In liberal society, consent alone can implicate others. Why the freedom to choose is at the core of the liberal conception of justice can be attributed to this desire to keep disagreements about morality out of the sphere of politics.

The liberal political order is not meant to be the expression of what the ideal person ought to be according to some doctrine about human nature, but rather an accommodation among people who may or may not hold different views about the good life. The fact that they may happen to hold similar conceptions of the good life entails the possibility of a closely knit community, but this remains a contingent factor. Individuals may be capable of agreeing on a conception of the good or of reaching a social consensus, but the respect for their autonomy precludes imposing upon them a particular life plan. Or, at the least, liberalism stresses the distinction between a public sphere where liberal principles of justice rule and a private sphere where shared ideals of the good life allow for deep attachments. To some extent, the question of people's identities and shared moral sense being shaped through communal membership remains beyond the scope of liberalism's claims. Not that it denies the importance of communal ties, but rather that it does not pretend to provide human beings with a world outlook. What liberalism instead provides is a system of rights and duties attached to citizenship.

The liberal project is, in that respect, quite attractive. Indeed, it recognizes individual rights as the concrete expression of a full citizenship for all. It stays away from the risky business of incorporating into the state the identity that is constitutive of a people. The aim of the great liberal struggles, from the separation of church and state to the bestowing of civil rights, was to dissociate the individual from the citizen, so to speak. Liberalism accounts for the person as a political being, with rights and duties attached to his or her public identity irrespective of that person's (changing) conception of the good, private identity, personal loyalties, and, we might add, irrespective of that person's communal membership.[3] The feudal notion of a differentiated citizenship, one that determines a person's status according to his belonging in a particular group, has no place in the modern discourse of democratic society.[4] A political doctrine that would ignore the distinction and mix the two realms together would likely lead to illiberal conclusions.

Derived from this definition of liberalism and its associated view of citizenship is the idea of state neutrality. The arguments for state neutrality sometimes rest on a belief that knowledge about the good life is unavailable to us, that there is no basis for choosing one way of life over another. If such is our inherent limit, then how can the state not be neutral? If, on the contrary, we believe that it is possible to discover our highest good, then surely the state ought not to coerce citizens if freedom is valued at all. In any case, the liberal state must be neutral in the face of multiple and differing conceptions of the good. The proper role of the state is not to opt for and pursue a particular view of the good life, for example evaluating and promoting virtue in its citizens. Ronald Dworkin argues that the state should treat individuals as equals, which presupposes an official neutrality amongst views of what the good life is:

> Since the citizens of a society differ in their conceptions [of the good life], the government does not treat them as equals if it prefers one conception to another, either because the officials believe that one is intrinsically superior, or because one is held by the more numerous or more powerful group.[5]

This kind of equality he believes to be the constitutive principle of liberalism. But if liberals proscribe the use of state power to enforce moral values, it is not because questions of morality are unimportant, as Rawls writes, but "because we think them too important and recognize that there is no way to resolve them politically".[6] And not only do we not agree on what the good life is, but even if we did we also tend to believe that the state is likely to distort or misfire, despite the best intentions.[7]

To what extent can (or ought) the state be morally neutral is a difficult question in itself. This kind of "moral disestablishment", as Neil MacCormick calls it, usually admits state intervention via criminal law where harm is done to individuals. State neutrality, coupled with some intervention to prevent harm,

> appeal[s] to the (moral) value of respecting persons as autonomous moral agents, and thus to the derivative value of protecting persons from invasions of their autonomy. [8]

He goes on to say that

> [s]tate powers may be and ought to be exercised so as to enforce moral requirements, but only those which are other-regarding duties of respect for persons, and only to the smallest extent necessary for securing to all the conditions of self-respect as autonomous beings. [9]

But as he observes, the principle of harm is itself a morally loaded concept, for it involves some idea of what interests are to be protected against harm. We can see how the deviation from state neutrality to state intervention is made easier with such fluid concepts as harm and morality. Joseph Raz, for example, goes further when he displaces state neutrality in favour of a view of the state that enables "individuals to pursue valid conceptions of the good and to discourage evil or empty ones". [10] Note how this is different from the directive that government action ought to be neutral between acceptable ends and unacceptable ones, that it should neither hinder nor help valid ideals more than reprehensible and offensive ones.

In spite of these differences among them, liberals agree that political regimes built around a single vision of the good life err in their conception of justice. This view is derived from a skepticism about the possibility of knowing the good, or from a belief that even if the good is known, it does not belong in the political realm. In any case, we must rise above our communal attachments to deliberate as equal citizens on the principles and institutions that guide society. This partly explains liberalism's committment to autonomy as a most fundamental good, that of being the author of one's life, and consequently of being free to make choices. Political arrangements which maximize autonomy—such as a system of individual rights—are therefore a central feature of liberal society and, as it will become clear, increasingly a central feature of Canadian society.

The recognition of rights neither begins nor ends with liberalism. Some views of the world that pre-date the liberal era acknowledged rights, and many of today's non-liberal ideologies share with liberals a full conception of rights. However, perhaps no other ideology has embraced rights to such an extent, making liberalism and rights seem natural companions. In our attempt to define the core values of liberalism, it is worth asking ourselves what rights are, bearing in mind Colin Wringe's point that

> a most fertile source of confusion and conflict regarding the rights of individuals is the assumption that a definition of a right can be given which is at once simple and informative, and that claims to rights which do not fit such a formula are to be rejected out of hand. [11]

A familiar formulation of rights adheres to the following structure: individual A has a right to X in relation to individual B, giving rise to B having a duty Y towards A. (A is the right-holder, B the duty-holder, X the object of the right, and Y the correlative duty.) The important point is that a right generally entails a corresponding duty from other persons or institutions to act (or to refrain from acting) toward the right-holder in accordance with the requirements of the right.[12] In *Utilitarianism*, John Stuart Mill defined a right in this way:

> When we call anything a person's right, we mean that he has a valid claim on society to protect him in the possession of it, either by the force of law, or by that of education and opinion. If he has what we consider a sufficient claim, on whatever account, to have something guaranteed to him by society, we say that he has a right to it. [13]

If I have a right against arbitrary detention, it entails that people and institutions have the duty of not detaining me arbitrarily, that they do not have the freedom to do so. As H. L. A. Hart puts it, "[t]o have a right entails having a moral justification for limiting the freedom of another person and for determining how he should act".[14] To assert a right is to assert that there is such a justification. "Rights are", in the words of Jan Narveson, "duty-creating properties".[15]

The relation between rights and duties viewed this way suggests that rights precede duties, that duties are inferred from rights. Rights and duties are not linked as if they were "two sides of the same coin", as

Joel Feinberg notes. [16] Where there is a right, there is a duty. But if rights imply duties, not all duties are derived from rights, which is to say that not all duties are duties of *justice*. This is a distinction Mill made:

> Justice implies something which it is not only right to do, and wrong not to do, but which some individual person can claim from us as his moral right. No one has a moral right to our generosity or beneficience, because we are not morally bound to practise those virtues towards any given individual. [17]

There are, for example, duties of benevolence, for which there are no clearly identifiable attached rights. Parents no doubt feel some kind of obligation to give their children love, though strictly speaking children do not have a right to this. But children do have a right against their parents injuring them, which entails a duty of justice on the part of parents. The relevant idea here is that not all moral considerations are to be expressed in the language of rights, either because they go beyond duties of justice or because they are of a nature not easily expressed in the language of rights. Critics of community rights, we shall see, sometimes argue that only individual rights entail a duty of justice, hence that communal claims have no place under this rubric, though they may be of some importance.

Another interesting characteristic of rights in a liberal society like Canada is that they are generally understood as being universal, as applying equally to everyone. They would exist in the same degree regardless of where one lives or who one is. This is reminiscent of the notion of human rights, which would involve matters of such importance that they ought to be taken seriously in any society.[18] The view that rights precede political society, that they originate in the state of nature, further serves to justify the universality of rights. Whether or not rights are recognized, they are said to exist and be meaningful. For example, if cultural diversity explains why some peoples do not recognize rights, it does not mean that the rights are non-existent. [19] This is an interesting question, for it bears upon the issue of community rights, as we shall see in chapter 3.

To be liberal, in short, is to believe that people ought to be left alone to think and do what they choose as long as no one is harmed in the process. That is why the state ought to treat us as citizens, as abstract political beings, and ought to be blind to the differences between people, blind to their respective identities. That is also why liberals cherish individual rights, for they say something about the moral relationship between citizens, what we should and should not do to each other as autonomous beings. As a general rule of action, liberals believe that individual rights ought to be respected, and that only an overriding moral concern may justify restrictions on rights. We always need a moral justification for limiting a right, that is, "it is always wrong unless some other moral consideration outweighs its wrongness". [20] Most Canadians find this congenial to their beliefs about the value of personal autonomy and the worth of their liberties. That is partly why rights-discourse has so quickly been able to occupy a central place in Canada's political culture. It also explains why those who speak of genuine community and communal goods have a hard time with the liberal view and its associated rights-talk. At the very least they have a hard time with this particular brand of liberalism—increasingly referred to as "procedural" liberalism.

Much of what I explore in this book hinges on the idea of community in liberal society. [21] As we just saw, liberalism offers us a vision of community which is largely grounded in the respect for autonomy and which proclaims the sanctity of individual rights. It is an appealing vision, yet we may wonder whether it properly considers the need for those goods that fashion our identity. What kind of goods am I talking about? This is not only a question of political theory, but a very real issue that must be examined when trying to make sense of language rights in Canada. For the problem is largely about a conflict between one vision of community that is growing out of the Charter culture, and another vision of community that better corresponds to our self-understandings as situated beings.

The list of things that could be considered "goods" is endless, varying in time and space. I may consider some object to be a good in the pursuit of my life project, while someone else with an equally rational plan of life will discount it. As Rawls explains, "once we establish that an object has the properties that it is rational for someone with a rational plan of life to want, then we have shown that it is good for him". [22] We can conceive a good as an end in itself which, as John Finnis says, makes intelligible instances of the human activity involved in its pursuit. There are goods which he believes to be the basic purposes of human action: life, knowledge, play, aesthetic experience, friendship, religion, and practical reasonableness (to choose and pursue our life plans in a free and responsible manner). These goods, he argues, are the first-order values from which other goods are derived:

> First, each [value] is equally self-evidently a form of good. Secondly, none can be analytically reduced to being merely an aspect of any of the others, or to being merely instrumental in the pursuit of any of the others. Thirdly, each one, when we focus on it, can reasonably be regarded as the most important. Hence there is no objective hierarchy amongst them. [23]

He may be wrong about his list, but in any case it gives an idea of what is meant by goods-as-ends. Other things we consider as goods are means to an end. To use Finnis' example, if knowledge is a basic end, then a sound brain is a means for the pursuit of knowledge. Rawls' primary goods fall in this category. They constitute what every person can be presumed to want in order to execute a rational plan of life: social primary goods such as liberties, opportunities, wealth and self-respect, and natural primary goods such as health, imagination and intelligence. [24] Here the goods are not primary in the sense of being basic ends, but primary because they are believed to be some of the necessary means to advance our aims, whatever these are.

So there are countless things we call "goods" because we see them as making up human action or giving it a purpose. The liberal community, as we examined above, provides us with a good that is most valued, that of autonomy: the freedom to be the author of our own lives in our own way. We tend to look upon this as evidence that liberal justice is the guardian of individual goods, understood as our most fundamental goods. Perhaps this assumes too quickly that there is a clear cut distinction between individual goods and communal goods. After all, goods are all communal insofar as our belief in their value comes from our belonging in a particular community. Many of our freedoms are individual goods to the extent that they need not be shared in order to be meaningful. Yet the fact that we find them meaningful in the first place is the result of our membership in the liberal community, with all the deep-rooted ideological beliefs that come with it. In a different time and place, they might not be considered goods at all, or at least might not hold the same rank in the hierarchy of values. Conversely, goods can be understood as being all individual since it is difficult to see how a community can enjoy anything, not being an entity in the modern sense. Since goods benefit individuals but have their source in community membership, they may be conceived as both individual and communal.

The distinction between individual goods and communal goods being somewhat tenuous, it should not come as a surprise that the notorious debate between individual rights and collective rights be even more confusing. It is often mistakenly perceived as a conflict between those most important things that we value as individuals and the tyranny of community dressed up in the language of rights. Needless to say, describing the issue in such simplistic terms detracts from the real question, which is whether there are goods whose worth escape liberal justice. Few will disagree that some goods are valuable to us because they are essential to our identity. Of course identity can be made to designate just about anything depending on one's perspective. But what I mean by identity here is that region of our personality which is shaped by belonging in a particular community and which says something about who we are, or who we *think* we are, and where we come from. Identity is the substance of the self that precedes our actions as autonomous beings. Charles Taylor writes that identity "is who we are, 'where we're coming from.' As such it is the background against which our tastes and desires and opinions and aspirations make sense." [25] Consider also how William Connolly sees it:

> My identity is what I am rather than what I choose, want, or consent to. It is the dense self from which choosing, wanting, and consenting proceed. Without that density, these acts could not occur; with it they are said to be mine. Our identity ... is what we are and the basis from which we proceed. [26]

Identity is a substantive value, not derived from autonomy, but prior to it. Taylor also notes how identity is acquired and defined through dialogue rather than through self-generation and solitary reflection. Identity makes little sense when it is understood as a purely individualistic notion. It is the product of an ongoing conversation with others, or as Michael Oakeshott would say, of an exploration into our community's inheritance and intimations. [27] If the *I* and the *we* are separate entities, they are nevertheless profoundly intertwined as they together form the complex facets of our identity. In this picture, we are beings made-up of something more than a thin autonomous self.

The suggestion is that our communality provides the material of our identity in the form of shared goods that cannot be experienced in isolation in any meaningful way. The good of culture, language, and sovereignty, to name only a few, cannot be experienced alone. Jeremy Waldron uses the example of conviviality to show that "[s]ome goods are not privately enjoyable because to enjoy them one must be doing so in the company of others and with the assurance that they are enjoying them as well". [28] In the same vein, Taylor speaks of those goods whose value comes from their being shared, not only things that "have value to me and to you", but things that "essentially have value to us".[29] Such communal goods have no meaning to an individual outside collective participation.

By constrast, Taylor notes how there are goods which are not available outside collective participation and so must be collectively provided, but which would have the same value for the individual alone were it possible to afford or obtain them alone. Security and welfare are such goods. The idea of welfare, Ronald Garet writes, is individualistic "in that the ultimate particle of satisfaction is the satisfaction of individual preferences" and social "in that the preferences are voiced collectively and addressed in the aggregate". [30] This is akin to the contractarian idea of having mutual, yet inherently solitary, interests. They may be voiced in the aggregate and apply to a collection of individuals, but they are not experienced and enjoyed as shared goods in the stronger sense.

Communal goods held in common can serve as a kind of marker of community membership, insofar as being a member involves participating in the enjoyment of such goods. It is the *sharing* of a common ethnicity or a common language that allows for a community formed of common purposes and ends. Robert Paul Wolff writes about an aspect of community as

> the reciprocal consciousness of a shared culture. It is not the culture itself; nor is it the purely private enjoyment which individuals may take in that culture. Rather, it is the mutual awareness on the part of each that there are others

sharing that culture, and that through such mutuality we are many together rather than many alone. [31]

Furthermore, the sharing of communal goods might reinforce what some have refered to as a sense of solidarity and a sense of significance. [32] Solidarity, understood as a feeling of togetherness, cohesion and belonging, is more likely to be stronger (I assume) where people share a good that is at the heart of their identity. Significance, taken as a feeling of achievement, fulfilment, and contribution to the whole, is also more likely to be present when people feel they have a part to play in the overall story—insofar as it is possible to count for something in a large-scale community. But for there to be a story in the first place, common meanings and understandings are at least necessary.

The point I wish to stress is the following. In Canada, we usually interpret our conflicts over language issues as an expression of an uncomfortable relationship between Québec and Canada, French Canadians and English-speaking Canadians. While it is true that some of these conflicts are rooted in the federal system and in the bi-national nature of the country, it is the tension between the two concurrent memberships described in this chapter that lies at the heart of the problem. It may very well be that liberalism, not Ottawa, poses the greatest threat to French Canada. What we have are two overlapping communities, one that is rooted in liberal values, another whose foundations rest on how we construe "who we are".[33] Both are, I suspect, intuitively appealing to Canadians. No one (I hope) wants to live in a society which only protects our personal autonomy. Nor does anyone (I'm sure) want to be treated as an heteronomous being. The challenge, therefore, is to rethink a political community that springs from our self-image as self-authored, yet situated, citizens.

Of course liberals know that communal ties and attachments go beyond the moral relationship involved in the mutual safeguarding of our personal autonomy. They understand that community is also built on a combination of shared traits such as a common ethnicity or language, and inter-subjective understandings and purposes derived from sharing that common ethnicity or language. They do not contest the claim that these aspects of community are a source of identity and, through a shared participation in seeking communal goods, a source of well-being. Yet all of this does not sit well with liberal justice.

Notes

1. John Rawls, "Justice as Fairness: Political not Metaphysical", *Philosophy and Public Affairs* 14, no. 3 (Summer 1985).

2. Richard Vernon, "Moral Pluralism and the Liberal Mind", in *Unity, Plurality and Politics*, ed. J. M. Porter and Richard Vernon (London: Croom Helm, 1986), 159.

3. See for example John Rawls, "Justice as Fairness: Political not Metaphysical", 242. Also see Charles Larmore, "Michael J. Sandel: Liberalism and the Limits of Justice", *The Journal of Philosophy* 81, no. 6 (1984): 340.

4. Will Kymlicka and Wayne Norman, "Return of the Citizen: A Survey of Recent Work on Citizenship Theory", *Ethics* 104 (January 1994): 352-381.

5. Ronald Dworkin, "Liberalism", in *Public and Private Morality*, ed. Stuart Hampshire (Cambridge: Cambridge University Press, 1978), 113-143.

6. Rawls, "Justice as Fairness: Political not Metaphysical", 230.

7. See Joseph Raz's discussion of this question in *The Morality of Freedom* (Oxford: Clarendon Press, 1986), 111.

8. Neil MacCormick, "Against Moral Disestablishment", in his *Legal Right and Social Democracy* (Oxford: Clarendon Press, 1982), 29.

9. MacCormick, "Against Moral Disestablishment", 37.

10. Raz, *The Morality of Freedom*, 133.

11. Colin A. Wringe, *Children's Rights: A Philosophical Study* (London: Routledge and Kegan Paul, 1981), 37.

12. I borrow this structure from Alan Gewirth, "The Epistemology of Human Rights", *Human Rights*, ed. Ellen Paul, Jeffrey Paul, and Fred Miller

(Oxford: Basil Blackwell, 1984), 1, and from Joel Feinberg, *Rights, Justice, and the Bounds of Liberty* (Princeton: Princeton University Press, 1980).

13.   John Stuart Mill, *Utilitarianism* (Toronto: Penguin Books, 1987), 326. For an interesting analysis of Mill's views on rights, see Tom Regan, *The Case for Animal Rights* (Berkely: The University of California Press, 1983), chapter 8.

14.   H. L. A. Hart, "Are There Any Natural Rights?", in *Theories of Rights*, ed. Jeremy Waldron (Oxford: Oxford University Press, 1984), 83.

15.   Jan Narveson, "Collective Rights?", *The Canadian Journal of Law and Jurisprudence* 4, no. 2 (July 1991): 330.

16.   Joel Feinberg, "The Nature and Value of Rights", in his *Rights, Justice, and the Bounds of Liberty* (Princeton: Princeton University Press, 1980), 149.

17.   Mill, *Utilitarianism*, 323.

18.   On the question of human rights, see Maurice Cranston, "Human Rights, Real and Supposed", in *Political Theory and the Rights of Man*, ed. D. D. Raphael (London: MacMillan, 1967).

19.   See Stuart M. Brown's discussion of this question in "Inalienable Rights", *The Philosophical Review* 64 (1955): 200.

20.   William K. Frankena, "Natural and Inalienable Rights", *The Philosophical Review* 64 (1955): 230.

21.   Although we might think that the idea of community is self-explanatory, there is actually little agreement over its meaning. Raymond Plant rightly notes that community can only be given a descriptive meaning against a particular ideological background. While it should be possible to provide a formal concept of community acceptable to all regardless of ideological commitments, he argues, such concept would have no operational use in political analysis. Moving beyond such a formal and empty concept, on the other hand, would produce a contestable conception again. This difficulty is not unique to the idea of community, as we shall see. For example, the formal "concept" of justice as the absence of arbitrariness in the distribution of rights and duties will agree with various "conceptions" of justice based on desert, or fairness, or need, or moral worth. The point is that we must be aware of the ideological shape that community takes, and therefore the beliefs and values that are understood to be at its core. See Raymond Plant, "Community: Concept, Conception, and Ideology", *Politics and Society* 8, no. 1 (1978): 83-88.

22.   John Rawls, *A Theory of Justice* (Cambridge: The Belknap Press of Harvard University Press, 1971), 399.

23.   John Finnis, *Natural Law and Natural Rights* (Oxford: Clarendon Press, 1980), 92, 60-62, 81-90.

24.   Rawls, *A Theory of Justice*, 62.

25.   Charles Taylor, "The Politics of Recognition", in *Multiculturalism and 'The Politics of Recognition'*, ed. Amy Gutmann (Princeton: Princeton University Press, 1993), 33. Also see by Taylor *The Malaise of Modernity* (Concord, Ont.: Anansi, 1991), 31-41; and "Atomism", in his *Philosophy and the Human Sciences* (Cambridge: Cambridge University Press, 1985), 208-209.

26.   William Connolly, "Identity and Difference in Liberalism", *Liberalism and the Good*, ed. R. Bruce Douglas, Gerald M. Mara, and Henry S. Richardson (New York: Routledge, 1990), 59.

27.   Michael Oakeshott, "Political Education", in his *Rationalism in Politics* (New York: Basic Books, 1962), 129.

28.   Jeremy Waldron, "Rights, Public Choice and Communal Goods", *Legal Theory Workshop Series* (Toronto: University of Toronto, 1986), 14.

29.   Charles Taylor, "Cross-Purposes: The Liberal-Communitarian Debate", in *Liberalism and the Moral Mind*, ed. Nancy L. Rosenblum (Cambridge, Ma.: Harvard University Press, 1989), 168.

30.   Ronald R. Garet, "Communality and Existence: The Rights of Groups", *Southern California Review* 56, no. 5 (July 1983): 1053.

31.   Robert Paul Wolff, *The Poverty of Liberalism* (Boston: Beacon Press, 1968), 187.

32.   See for example David B. Clark, "The Concept of Community: A Re-Examination", *The Sociological Review* 21, no. 3, New Series (August 1973): 404.

33.   We must also remember that unlike the liberal community, the community of identity is usually not a matter of choice where individuals come together into a voluntary association to pursue parallel interests. In this case, community membership is not primarily voluntary as it is more likely to be inherited than chosen and, by the same token, less likely to be revised or reconsidered. Since communal membership of this kind is not the result of a contractual obligation, so is joining or leaving a community not just a matter of making or breaking a contract.

2

What's Wrong with Liberal Society?

To ask what could be wrong with liberal society at first seems counter-intuitive. After all, liberal principles articulate well the widespread opinions about what the demands of justice are, and consequently have become central to our political culture, most notably with rights-discourse. And since those who speak of the good of community will hear no objections from liberals, there seems to be no need to oppose community and liberalism in such a dualistic fashion, as if liberalism was not itself a conception of community, or as if communitarians did not share liberal values. We should not foreclose the possibility of conceiving community in holistic terms, as a place where the fundamental values of autonomy and identity can meet, and where both can find proper protection in a system of rights. Anything else, it will be said, inevitably leads to moral mistakes, the kinds that are too often made when judging language rights in Canada.

Still, we must ask to what extent liberalism can recognize community without compromising its core values. We must also ask whether all the goods that are worthy to human beings can find adequate protection in a liberal system of rights, or whether some of them are squeezed out of the system altogether. Attempts have been made to show the weaknesses of the liberal tradition in providing a plausible view of community. In response to these critics, some liberals have re-examined the foundations of liberal theory with the aim of showing the critics wrong in their assessment of it, thus proposing new ways of integrating community undiminished into liberal frameworks of justice. Have they succeeded?

We can begin by noting that liberals do not deny the reality of the context in which one is born and the inescapable ties that this entails. It would be a mistake to imply that liberals like Rawls do not accept the importance of community, for they agree that it is partly through communal membership that individuals can shape and make choices among the various options open to them. Liberals generally admit that even in a pluralistic society, non-voluntary communal memberships shape personal identity and cannot be avoided. Only, these attachments must not enter the public sphere where citizens are equally free and capable to choose their life plans.

The problem with this view is that it factors out some aspects of community membership as being insignificant when the terms and rules of liberal justice are to be deliberated upon. Individualistic conceptions of the good dominate and preclude shared community values that are central to one's identity. Some communal goods (e. g. language) become more difficult to pursue within liberal frameworks of justice since their realization could require forms of cooperation—and forms of restrictions—that might be inconsistent with the principles of justice thus chosen. The resulting views on rights are inherently individualistic and cannot appreciate the pursuit of communal goods other than derivatively. It is almost as if our communality is irrelevant from a moral standpoint. Rawls, for example, wants to account for the intrinsic value of community, but only once a conception of justice that is admittedly individualistic is worked out first.[1] As a result of undervaluing communal attachments, his theory precludes the possibility of accounting for them as first-order goods. The ensuing principles of justice and terms of social cooperation do not account fully for community. A further consequence is that they are ill-equiped to deal fairly with the inevitable tensions that arise when actions to promote a communal identity encounter liberal justice.

At first glance it is questionable whether community can truly be included in liberal frameworks of justice.[2] The communitarian critique of liberalism is instructive in that regard. Since the early eighties, so-called communitarians have centered on the claim that liberal theories of justice neglect to take seriously the social features that are constitutive of a person's identity. We saw how liberals hold that the principles of justice determining rights and duties and regulating the distribution of social and economic benefits should not presuppose any particular conception of the good life. But the liberal theory of justice, communitarians charge, is mistakenly understood as a framework of fundamental rights which is prior to the conceptions of the various shared goods persons may have. The theoretical constructions such as Rawls' theory of justice therefore appeal to an unacceptable view of the self as "unencumbered" by social circumstances and attachments. As Michael Sandel puts it, the view of the unencumbered self denies the "possibility of membership in any community bound by moral ties antecedent to choice" [3]. It denies the possibility of a community that is constitutive of one's identity and allows only for supposedly chosen attachments. Hence one problem with liberalism is that its conception of persons as authors of their own lives conflicts with our self-understandings as beings whose identities are tied to the community. To put it differently, communitarians believe that we discover our ends embedded in a social context, rather than choosing these as unencumbered selves, and so they object to the idea of a self free from the social features of identity.

The liberal counter charges are interesting, not only for their attempt to show how communitarians fail to undermine liberalism, but also for their reassessment of the liberal view of community. Will Kymlicka, for example, suggests that the communitarian critique is ill-founded, for it misunderstands what liberalism is all about. Liberalism, he argues, is about the freedom to question the beliefs that form our vision of the good life. This is why liberals like Rawls accord priority to liberty, not on the grounds that our ends are determined presocially, but rather on the grounds that our interests are formed within a social context in which individuals acquire and revise their ends. "The liberal view is not that we can perceive a self prior to its ends", he writes, but rather that our ends are open to possible re-examinations upon critical reflection, yet always as selves who remain encumbered by a social system of values which underwrites our beliefs and actions.[4] In other words, no *particular* end is given with the self, but there is always *some* end.

Reassessing the importance of community in liberal theory, Kymlicka still maintains that cultural membership must occupy a central place in our society, for it is only within a secure cultural context that one can make significant choices.[5] Don Lenihan sums up his argument:

Kymlicka's argument is that cultural membership is a precondition for
meaningful individual choice, and meaningful individual choice is crucial for
the good life. As a marketplace for opportunities, a culture offers its members
an adequate range of materials from which they may select in order to
construct coherent and meaningful life-plans for themselves. Without this
context, we would have no sense of value, no appreciation of what anything
was worth. [6]

Viewed this way, culture is the context in which individuals form their
beliefs and select their conception of the valuable life; thus, choosing
meaningful ends depends upon the existence of a rich cultural
environment. However, the cultural context will have to be a context
of choice: it will have to allow individuals the freedom to endorse or
reject the character of their community and its way of life. Cultural
membership, Kymlicka writes, must not undermine "the very reason
we had for being concerned with cultural membership—that it allows
for meaningful individual choices".[7] He therefore concludes that
"concern for the cultural structure as a context of choice ... accords
with, rather than conflicts with, the liberal concern for our ability and
freedom to judge the value of our life-plans".[8] In the end, freedom of
choice is regarded as being prior to the ties that bind us to our
community. Community must remain commensurable with liberty.

As we can see, what underlies Kymlicka's compromise is a strategy
to reconcile the value of community with the value of free choice. But
in order to achieve this, he must opt for a definition of culture which
has been emptied of its substance, of its character. Indeed, he draws a
distinction between the *character* of a community, namely its values,
beliefs, norms, etc., and the *function* of community as a context of
choice. On this view, the claims that a community would make to
protect its character would have to be subordinate to its function as a
context of choice required to maximize autonomy.

Joseph Raz's theory looks at the issue of community in liberalism
from another   perspective. Community is valued because of its
contribution to the good life, to human well-being, and is essential to
attaining an autonomous life. To this end, he argues that we should
have a sufficient range of acceptable, or morally valuable, options open
to us, some of which require the existence of communal goods which
are subject to the community's control, or at least to social

conventions. Promoting these communal goods would therefore not constitute a limit on personal autonomy. On the contrary. And since the options available to us ought to be worthy ones—otherwise they would not contribute to the realization of autonomy—then state intervention which promotes worthy choices over evil ones is morally desirable. Thus Raz hopes to answer communitarian critiques by presenting a view of community as something essential to realizing personal autonomy, while remaining liberal by deriving the good of community from the ultimate value of autonomy. It is, he writes, "an endeavour to argue for a liberal morality on non-individualistic grounds". [9]

This kind of liberal morality, according to Margaret Moore, is somewhat incoherent when it claims that the value of autonomy is derived from its role in fostering community, but that autonomy is the ultimate value on which community is to be assessed. [10] This is a tricky aspect of the modified liberal view. It wishes to recognize values that are prior to autonomy, values on which our autonomous choices can be gauged, but that would jeopardize the substantive character of autonomy and possibly justify its subordination to such values. About Kymlicka's position, Moore writes that

> what determines which community conceptions are acceptable and which are not ... are traditional *liberal* principles, which protect individual autonomy, understood in terms of a sphere of action attached to each individual in which interference is unjustified. It is hard to see how this theory can credibly claim to meet the objections of communitarians, who criticize liberalism on the grounds (a) that it gives value only to the exercise of autonomy, and not to substantive values which are also important aspects of the good life, and (b) that it is unable to give importance to the value of the community, which is also important to human flourishing. [11]

So can liberalism adequately account for cultural membership and community? For one thing, even the revised liberal view only defends the proposition that community, ultimately any worthy community, is central to autonomous choice *if it promotes autonomy*; otherwise, communities have very little ground to claim protection. They must not defeat their purpose, which is the promotion of autonomous choices. This is all very consistent with the belief in a plurality of sometimes opposing conceptions of the good, and that for this reason we must respect the freedom of persons to make their own choices. Liberals wish to recognize the importance of the cultural matrix to making significant choices, but must also defend these choices in the face of potentially restrictive communal practices. Lenihan puts it well when he writes that liberals (like Kymlicka) fear "the loss of a firm foundation for both the self's right and power to act according to self-imposed, rationally justified, standards of morality", but that "hanging on too tightly to autonomy steers one away from, not toward, a deeper understanding of the moral significance of cultural membership".[12]

Perhaps all of this meets our deep-felt sentiments about accepting the good of community while avoiding the temptation of group tyranny. Or does it? Is there a sense in which the very existence of communities does not accord with maximizing individual choices? A common and thorny instance of this is when a community's views of what the valuable way of life is forecloses children's ability to partake in the dominant society and eventually join it.[13] It is likely that the education a child receives in a (marginal) traditional community diminishes his or her chances of making certain life plans, at least those that are valued in mainstream society. On the other hand, we cannot a priori reject the validity of the claim that that community must restrict some opportunities for its members on the rationale that it must reproduce itself. This points to a difficult issue, for if liberalism accepted that community is considered an essential good, then it would also have to accept that the survival of some communities calls for limits on individual choices. It cannot, since such limits would mean approving that community members be treated as instruments serving the imperatives of their community's survival.

But there are several problems here. By opposing limitations on individual choices, does not liberalism likely foreclose the opportunity of an individual to choose that traditional way of life during adulthood, having been educated to perform in technical occupations and socialized in leading the fast and materialist life? Along similar lines, Michael McDonald writes:

> This not only threatens the existence of some groups, but it paradoxically diminishes individual choice while increasing it; for the creation of a new set of options for the child either eliminates the earlier option of remaining within the traditional culture or dramatically raises its costs. [14]

Furthermore, freedom of choice can lead more vulnerable communities to disappear or integrate into the dominant society. Particular values and conceptions of the good, and even whole communities, may be lost in the process, thus reducing the actual number of alternatives for future generations. Restricting choices in a community, the argument goes, could therefore prevent the loss of alternative choices in the long run and make them available to future generations. Put differently, when the liberal principle of choice is taken to its extreme, it eventually undermines the conditions in which significant choices can be exercised. In response to this critique, one could say that the charge of inconsistency does not hold since the liberal principle of maximizing choices still aims at expanding rather than deliberately contracting the range of possible alternatives. But this standpoint is nonetheless partly self-defeating in effect: it decreases the reasonable chances that a traditional way of life will be chosen once all alternatives have been examined and, what is more, reduces the number of alternatives for future generations.

Liberal society operates on the grounds that people have the rights of association and dissociation, that groups ought to be freely created and freely questioned, and thus supports a set of individual rights which partly serve this function. But as Michael McDonald rightly notes, modern mass culture has had a destructive effect on some marginal communities, and the exercise of individual rights has done little to prevent their disintegration. "For such societies", he writes, "there is a kind of Humpty Dumpty effect; once such a community is shattered it cannot be put back together again". [15]

The problem appears most acute in education where the transmission of values to children is often justified on paternalistic grounds. Amy Gutmann suggests that "if there are certain primary goods that adults would choose to have had provided to them as children, then we might justify paternalistic interventions that supply these goods". [16] If children have a right to certain primary goods, then parents and the state have paternalistic duties towards them. According to Gutmann, one such parental duty includes allowing children to choose from among a range of conceptions of the good life that differ from the parents' own conception or from that of their community.

This does not mean that parents cannot forbid their children to perform actions which are judged uncongenial to their sense of the good life or to their system of values. For instance "parents certainly have a right ... to forbid their children to eat pork within their home", but "they also have the duty to allow their children to be exposed to the knowledge that eating pork is considered a reasonable way of life by many other people".[17] Transmitting a particular way of life to one's children, it would seem, goes hand in hand with transmitting to them the knowledge of alternative ways of life. We can see that the standard of paternalism here consists in maximizing choices for children and educating them for an autonomous life.

What if this parental duty is not followed by parents? Gutmann's answer is that the state has the right to impose some level of education despite the parents' desires (although the question of how much compulsory education is acceptable remains open) because education allows children to realize their freedom to choose. She admits there are grounds for respecting parents' values since state education itself is not neutral and favours *some* view of the good life over others. But for Gutmann the problem is not so much *whose* values should be imposed, but rather *what* values ought to be imposed. Here the liberal principle of maximizing choices resurfaces as the chief criterion, for "[w]e are required to choose those [values] that are most neutral among competing conceptions of the good, standards that expand rather than contract a child's future ability to exercise meaningful choice".[18] The state therefore has the duty to guarantee that every child acquires equal citizenship through education.

So according to the modified liberal view, children should inherit their parents' and community's way of life as well as the knowledge of alternative ways of life. The problem, however, is that if their heritage happens to coincide with mainstream culture, they will more likely hold on to it, whereas if they inherit a marginal way of life, they will probably succumb to, or "choose", mainstream culture. We can imagine a mother who has the right to make her daughter wear her community's distinctive dress, but also the duty to inform her that other people dress differently, say by showing her fashion magazines. When she becomes an adult, the daughter will then be free to choose alternative ways of dressing, question communal practices and even reconsider her membership in the community. If this satisfies the liberal, the community in question might raise the point that the mother ought to restrict her daughter's access to such fashion magazines in order to avoid envy. In other words, they might argue that children's education should not aim at widening the range of choices if this means that the community will later be faced with losses in membership. Thus there is some appeal to the idea that fragile communities cannot permit the maximization of choices while trying to strengthen allegiance and conformity, especially where group coherence is threatened by the larger society. The "liberating" effect of liberalism brings people closer to the boundaries that separate their community from dominant society where communal values and practices are most vulnerable. There, some would say, communities cannot always afford to be liberal.

As a general rule of action, liberal education insures the greatest range of reasonable choices for children when they become adults. Or at the least, the transmission of a communal way of life should be in accordance with maximizing autonomous choices. This poses real difficulties. Given that one's identity is partly rooted in one's community and its distinct values, how is the good of community to be transmitted? Normal processes of socialization and ideological forces will serve that function where the community has a considerable power of attraction to a majority of people. But in cases where a community holds a marginal position relative to mainstream culture, maximizing the range of reasonable choices through education may erode the community insofar as opting out becomes an attractive alternative. McDonald puts it succinctly: "Collective autonomy for the minority will be diminished in order to advance the autonomy of individual members of the minority".[19] These examples show how a strict separation between citizenship and communal membership works at the expense of the latter, since the provisions for acquiring autonomy through a set of rights attached to one's citizenship may contribute to the demise of the communal matrix in which identity is shaped. As Joseph Pestieau writes:

> It is not enough to celebrate the Constitution and to guarantee rights to individuals to make fellow citizens out of them. They must find the roots of their adhesion to the liberal democratic state within their own traditions. They

need to be integrated into a community and to be part of a culture in which
they feel at home in order to accept others' differences and to be sure of their
own identity. The liberal democratic state is playing with fire if it cannot
acknowledge their needs... [20]

While on the subject of liberal education, it is worth noting that if
the revised liberal view agrees that for individuals to flourish they must
live in *some* community, that does not automatically answer why there
is a case for preserving *one's* community and transmitting it to future
generations. [21] It is one thing to argue that a cultural context, any
cultural context, will do. But why do we insist on transmitting our
own culture? Perhaps if we believe in the worth of our community to
our well-being, then it is a natural impulse to preserve its integrity and
pass on its values to our children. One line of argument would be that
we care about our offspring because we identify their interests with our
own, and hence future generations have claims on us in the same way
that we can claim a particular communal good in the present.[22] A
variation of this argument would be that people have interests in what
happens after their death, and thus may attach a legitimate interest in
passing on the community's goods to the next generations.[23] How far
parents and communities are justified in restricting choices on those
grounds shows just how tangled the question of justice between
generations is. There is no easy answer to the question, to be sure. But
Robert Paul Wolff offers a convincing one: it is the mutuality of
awareness, he writes,

> which makes participation in one's own traditions, however meager they may
> be, more satisfying than observation of the rituals of others, no matter how
> elaborate and aesthetically excellent. A man must be odd indeed who prefers
> always to be the accidental guest at another's family gathering! [24]

We can see how there are difficulties in accepting the good of
community without compromising one of the core values of liberalism,
that of autonomous choice. Liberalism is required to account for
community in order to provide individuals with the communal goods
that are essential to leading a worthy life. But the problem comes from
the initial reasoning behind liberal theory which cannot fully integrate
claims about the value of community. The principles of liberal justice
are likely to reflect a view in which the conditions for community

remain contingent upon personal choice, where the ability for individuals to choose and change their way of life is respected. This can in turn undermine a community's attempts to survive and grow. Liberal education is a delicate illustration of this problem, as it does not always foster the survival of vulnerable communities in a context of mass acculturation. There is *some* sense to the idea that the reproduction of communities sometimes does not accord with the maximization of individual choices, especially when it comes to the promotion and transmission of a communal identity. It is an uncomfortable situation for liberals, to be sure, but one that must be addressed nonetheless.

There is a more general point to be made, however. In construing the thesis that individuals ought to be authors of their own lives, along with a set of corresponding rights that foster individual development, liberals fail to account properly for the preservation of the context in which communal goods are fostered, goods which give meaning and substance to our identity. However appealing the liberal view is, the primacy of autonomy over other values as a foundation for modern society leads to political principles that can impose contraints on the promotion of worthy goods which, along with autonomy, are also central to our well-being. Of course liberals can adjust the parameters of autonomy to include the need for community, but they needlessly avoid the full recognition of other substantive values that contribute to human well-being, such as the value of identity.

Liberals give priority to autonomy and to independent judgment and hence pose conditions to the acceptance of community. Yet do we not surrender some autonomy to community as a major determinant of human action? Does not community partly subsume our subjectivity as distinct persons and source of our own reasons? That is not to say that human beings are mere instruments of community, inevitably carried by its superior force and limiting our capacity to influence positively the course of events. The view that communities ought to be treated as moral agents, just like individuals, does not sit well with modernity. Asserting that the reality of communities commands respect in the *same* way the reality of individuals does lead to an impasse. But these problematic assumptions bear little resemblance to what is being argued here: the belief that our constitutive communality must be fully recognized in liberal society or else we will be left with morally impoverished lives. The hard question, as we will see in the next chapter, is what this means for rights-talk.

Some will object that even if such arguments were correct, they would not apply to French Canada today. Surely Québec is a modern industrial society whose vulnerability does not come near that of Aboriginal communities, or of minority sects like the Hutterites or Old Order Amish. But the point of raising the above cases is to draw attention to the knot in liberal theory. Policies which aim at promoting and transmitting the French language must face the same ideological obstacles. As we shall see, the fact remains that market forces, mass acculturation and hegemonic projects together work against French Canada under the cover of liberal ideology.

The procedural version of liberalism I have outlined poses an additional problem that pervades debates on language rights in French Canada. It has to do with the conflict between the politics of "universalism", largely derived from this version of liberalism, and the politics of "difference", derived from a recognition of identity. Charles Taylor explains how the politics of universalism is a protest against differentiated citizenship, one with first-class and second-class citizens. Its emphasis on equal civil rights, for example, reflects difference-blind principles—the view that the state should not discriminate on the basis of how individuals differ. The politics of difference, on the other hand, reflect a desire to have one's distinct identity recognized, rather than ignored. As Taylor notes, initial demands for universal equality have, paradoxically, shifted to the politics of difference:

> The politics of difference is full of denunciations of discrimination and refusals of second-class citizenship. This gives the principle of universal equality a point of entry within the politics of dignity. But once inside, as it were, its demands are hard to assimilate to that politics. For it asks that we give acknowledgment and status to something that is not universally shared. Or, otherwise put, we give due acknowledgment only to what is universally present—everyone has an identity—through recognizing what is peculiar to each. The universal demand powers an acknowledgment of specificity. [25]

These demands, he goes on to say, are not for temporary measures that will take us back to pure difference-blindness—as is the objective of the reverse discrimination involved in affirmative action—but rather for the permanent maintenance of these differences.

We can see how these two positions conflict. Those who believe in difference-blindness view special recognition as a form of discrimination offensive to equal dignity. But as Taylor points out, those who wish to see their identity recognized charge that what is taken to be neutral difference-blindness in fact conceals the hegemony of majoritarian culture, "a particularism masquerading as the universal". [26]

Procedural liberalism is problematic for community. It is a problem because of its insistence that conceptions of the good life are irrelevant, and must remain irrelevant, to the sphere of politics. By abstracting the self from its "thick" identity, it ends up construing principles of justice that are inherently individualistic, as the primacy of personal autonomy attests. The ensuing political system is one which privileges individual rights and which on the surface appears neutral. That is all well for members of the majority, but is cold comfort for those whose communal identity is steadily eroded.

It is a problem because of its built-in individualism. Robert Nisbet wrote in that regard that "most of our difficulties with the philosophy of individualism at the present time come from our unconscious efforts to make the ethical aspect of individualism remain evocative when we have ceased to hold to the psychological and sociological premises of this philosophy". [27] Our view about freedom and creativity, he argues, should no longer be that which is based upon an emancipation from community interdependences, when these were thought of as repressing individual reason. Rather, exploring the ways in which our personality flourishes *within* community, not against it, allows us to rediscover the "contexts of individuality", as he puts it. We could say that the liberal separation between citizenship and communal attachments stands on this ideological discrepancy between the reality of our social existence and the atomistic representation of the self.

In conclusion to this chapter, I can anticipate a powerful criticism of communitarian arguments, such as the one H. N. Hirsch bluntly makes: "that the longing for community is a chimera—romantic, naive, and, in the end, illiberal and dangerous". [28] By ignoring the separation between the political and the civil spheres, he argues, communitarians fuse our psychological identifications with our political status, they confuse membership and citizenship. Furthermore, strong community does nothing to solve the most urgent problems of the day. On the contrary, it creates many of them by excluding non-members to preserve its homogeneity and by fostering a system of moral education to maintain its integrity. In short, community and liberalism are incompatible.

While it is true that despite the best intentions oratory flights on community sometimes invoke the troubling image of patriarchal or theocratic societies, it will become clear in the next chapters that such a conclusion need not be made. Claims to the promotion of our communality, albeit more moderate claims, are not only defensible but can remain consistent with liberal values. It is always an uneasy mix, to be sure, but a necessary one if the reconfiguration of citizenship is going to be meaningful to us as we grapple with the demands of modernity. To this end, one of the first obstacles to surmount is a faulty discourse on rights.

Notes

1.   Rawls, *A Theory of Justice*, 264.

2.   On how this question relates specifically to Rawls' theory of justice, see Vernon Van Dyke, "Justice as Fairness: For Groups?", *The American Political Science Review* 69, no. 2 (1975): 607.

3.   Michael Sandel, "The Procedural Republic and the Unencumbered Self", *Political Theory* 12, no. 1 (February 1984): 87. Also by Sandel see "Justice and the Good", in *Liberalism and its Critics* (Oxford: Basil Blackwell, 1984). See also Alasdair MacIntyre, "The Virtues, the Unity of a Human Life and the Concept of a Tradition", in *Liberalism and Its Critics*. An interesting discussion of the liberal-communitarian debate is found in Daniel Bell, *Communitarianism and Its Critics* (Oxford: Clarendon Press, 1993). Also see Amy Gutmann, "Communitarian Critics of Liberalism", *Philosophy and Public Affairs* 14, no. 3 (1985).

4.　　Will Kymlicka, *Liberalism, Community, and Culture* (Oxford: Clarendon Press, 1989), 53.

5.　　Kymlicka, *Liberalism, Community, and Culture*, 169.

6.　　Donald Lenihan, "Liberalism and the Problem of Cultural Membership: A Critical Study of Kymlicka", *The Canadian Journal of Law and Jurisprudence* 4, no. 2 (July 1991): 407.

7.　　Kymlicka, *Liberalism, Community, and Culture*, 172.

8.　　Kymlicka, *Liberalism, Community, and Culture*, 167.

9.　　Joseph Raz, as quoted by Robert P. George, "The Unorthodox Liberalism of Joseph Raz", *The Review of Politics* 53, no. 4 (Fall 1991): 658.

10.　　Margaret Moore, "Liberalism and the Ideal of the Good Life", *The Review of Politics* 53, no. 4 (Fall 1991): 687-688.

11.　　Moore, "Liberalism and the Ideal of the Good Life", 685.

12.　　Donald Lenihan, "Liberalism and the Problem of Cultural Membership: A Critical Study of Kymlicka", 419.

13.　　On the difficult question of education in marginal communities, see L. S. Lustgarten, "Liberty in a Culturally Plural Society", in *Of Liberty*, ed. A. Phillips Griffiths (Cambridge: Cambridge University Press, 1983).

14.　　Michael McDonald, "Should Communities Have Rights? Reflections on Liberal Individualism", *The Canadian Journal of Law and Jurisprudence* 4, no. 2 (July 1991): 236.

15.　　McDonald, "Should Communities Have Rights? Reflections on Liberal Individualism", 230.

16.　　Amy Gutmann, "Children, Paternalism, and Education", *Philosophy and Public Affairs* 9, no. 4 (1980): 340.

17.　　Gutmann, "Children, Paternalism, and Education", 353.

18.　　Gutmann, "Children, Paternalism, and Education", 350.

19.　　McDonald, "Should Communities Have Rights? Reflections on Liberal Individualism", 236.

20. Joseph Pestieau, "Minority Rights: Caught Between Individual Rights and Peoples' Rights", *The Canadian Journal of Law and Jurisprudence* 4, no. 2 (July 1991): 368.

21. Brian Barry, "Self-Government Revisited", in *The Nature of Political Theory*, ed. David Miller and Larry Siedentop (Oxford: Clarendon Press, 1983), 149.

22. For a similar argument, see D. Clayton Hubin, "Justice and Future Generations", *Philosophy and Public Affairs* 6, no. 1 (1976): 70-83.

23. See Barry, "Self-Government Revisited", 145-153.

24. Wolff, *The Poverty of Liberalism*, 186.

25. Taylor, "The Politics of Recognition", 39.

26. Taylor, "The Politics of Recognition", 44.

27. Robert A. Nisbet, *The Quest for Community: A Study in the Ethics of Order and Freedom* (New York: Oxford University Press, 1953), 225.

28. H. N. Hirsch, "The Threnody of Liberalism: Constitutional Liberty and the Renewal of Community", *Political Theory* 14, no. 13 (August 1986): 424.

3

Making Sense of Community Rights

Vague invocations of collective rights often obscure the implications that come with claiming a right and the reasons for taking individual rights seriously. Perhaps this should not be surprising, for although the notion captures some of our convictions about the value of community, it can render rights-talk unintelligible. That is why many in Canada believe that collective rights should be rejected out of hand. Among Canadian political philosophers, too, discussions on community rights have showed how puzzling the conceptual dimension can be and the need to tidy up the whole language of rights. It seems that one of the underlying difficulties is to determine the class of subjects that qualify as right-holders. Living human beings obviously come to mind, but so may dead people, animals, and trees. How about communities? Is it both sound and useful to talk of community rights? It is an important question given the place that collective rights now occupy in Canadian rights-discourse. The underlying dispute is whether those goods that embody deep attachments receive enough recognition in liberal frameworks of rights.

We may begin by noting that any claim must be validated in order to be duly recognized as a right. This condition is especially important when it comes to justifying community rights, given the suspicions they arouse among many Canadians. On the one hand, it is not always clear what we have rights to, for they relate to different views about what kinds of interests justify holding others duty-bound. To debate whether we should have a right to a decent standard of living, or to a clean environment, or to access to culture, is to debate the relative importance of these interests. On the other hand, there are instances when it makes no sense to talk of someone or something being a right-holder—whatever they have a right to. Here the question is not about the object of the right, but about the nature of the claimant. For a claim to be valid, both ends must be justified.

As far as the western world goes, it is usually believed that only those entities that have an *inherent* value can be right-holders. A necessary condition, though not a sufficient one, for holding others duty-bound is to be a subject with an inherent value, hence a distinct source of valid claims. That is why human beings more immediately qualify, while trees do not. I will take this as a premise, not so much because human beings share certain attributes, such as the capacity to experience pleasure and pain, but because it is a presupposition whose moral relevance I cannot doubt. By extension, those things that do not have an inherent value, though they may be valuable, cannot be right-holders in the strict sense.

Some will interject that such a premise for construing rights is far too individualistic, for it rests on the assumption that only individuals have an inherent value, that only they can be distinct sources of valid claims. That communities can experience a we-ness shows evidence of some objective identity, they will say, and justifies treating them as "selves" with the rights that come with being self-determined and autonomous.[1] Otherwise the worth of communal claims will merely be derivative of the value we place on individuals.

Although such a perspective has the advantage of offering a tidy way of conceiving community rights, it is hard to fathom how communities could be right-holders in the same way individuals are. If a community could bear rights, it would mean that it can sustain interests of its own, be the source of its own worth and, as a consequence, can hold its individual members duty-bound to respect its claims. A community could claim a right against outside interference on the grounds that its actions are *self*-regarding even if they have undesirable effects on the lives of its members! Michael Hartney makes a clear distinction between the two positions:

> The important point to be made is that, whatever their views on these controversial matters, people generally believe that communities are important because of their contribution to the well-being of individuals. Such a view is part of what might be called *value-individualism*: only the lives of individual human beings have ultimate value, and collective entities derive their value

from their contribution to the lives of individual human beings. The opposite theory we might call *value-collectivism*: the view that a collective entity can have value independently of its contribution to the well-being of individual human beings. Such a position is counter-intuitive, and the burden of proof rests on anyone who wishes to defend it. [2]

The ideas behind value-collectivism belong to pre-modern organic conceptions of community. A more acceptable line of argument is to say that if a community has interests, they are ultimately reducible to the interests of its members. [3] No one disputes communities are valuable and collective interests are real, only these are indubitably derivative of the value and interests of individuals. To say that there are things we value because they constitute the core of our collective personality, to say that community is worthy, need not imply that the community has gained an inherent value over and above that of individuals. The individual members are those who have an inherent value, and only on this basis are they distinct sources of valid claims. Rights are meant to secure goods to individuals as moral agents, not to some other entity.

A sound justification of community rights would therefore have to avoid any intimation that communities are right-holders in this strong sense. But even some of the justifications for community rights consistent with value-individualism rest on shaky grounds. For example, it is sometimes argued that if someone or some institution has a duty to secure a communal good, the duty could not be grounded in one person's interests alone, but only on the interests of a collectivity of individuals who benefit from the right. In other words, far-reaching duties could not be justified for the sake of one person's interests. Community rights, on this view, are correlative of far-reaching duties. They are grounded in the idea that the duties they involve could not possibly rest on one individual's interest, but would have to be based on the interests of the people who together make up the community. [4] Where I think this argument falters is that the satisfaction of all goods, whether individual or communal, can potentially impose far-reaching demands on other people. To be sure, that some rights impose far-reaching duties may explain why they are often claimed collectively. But the provision of individual goods can also sometimes involve far-reaching demands, such as the duties involved in the fulfilment of welfare and environmental rights. Furthermore, to associate community rights with far-reaching duties leaves the impression that the communal goods in question are not sufficiently important to be justified on the interest of a single individual. If we follow this approach, it is not the urgency of the moral consideration that matters as a justifying base, but rather the number of claimants involved. Community rights improperly become the right of the many.

Other accounts tend to associate the public management of a resource or of some good with the exercise of a community right. For instance, some speak of Indian band councils whose power to control traditional resources in the name of community members is, in their opinion, evidence of a collective right.[5] I would agree that community representatives are better placed to manage a valuable resource, one that is central to the identity of the whole community. In that sense, they are the trustee of their members' rights. But it does not entail that the right to such a communal good is a community right. There are a number of individual goods (e. g. a minimum standard of living) that give rise to individual rights (e. g. welfare rights), but which nonetheless must be managed by the community (e. g. compulsory redistribution of resources). That the supplying of such goods might sometimes be controlled by the community does not mean collective rights are involved.

One way to bypass some of these difficulties in justifying collective rights is to regard communities as legal persons and therefore grant them rights persons would be entitled to have. Since we have no trouble speaking of rights for individuals, then let's look upon communities as individuals. Collective entities would be like legal persons, having the rights and duties associated with a legal personality, distinct from that of its "natural" members —not unlike corporations, which have the legal capacity to own property, incur debts, and even be convicted of crimes. Jeremy Waldron suggests for example that communities could be considered individuals from that point of view, that "[t]he French-speaking community in Canada can be considered as an individual vis-à-vis the federal government, other language groups and so on".[6] Vernon Van Dyke makes a similar point when he writes that communities "exist in the same sense that corporations do".[7] Both wish to reject organic views of community without falling prey to interpretations that reduce community to the sum of its members, and so are tempted to call upon group-personhood as a way out of this dilemma.

I think it unhelpful, however, to have recourse to group-personhood as a strategy to fit community into the framework of individual rights. From a legalistic point of view there may be some sense to the idea that communities can hold rights by virtue of their personhood. There may be cases where communities should be considered legal persons so as to facilitate representation in legal procedures, especially where liability is concerned. There might even be cases where communities are the trustees of their members' rights, especially when the rights involve goods which can only be collectively provided. But since it is impossible to conceive groups as persons other than by analogy, we need to go beyond the semantics and ask the real question, namely if a community can truly bear rights. To answer "no", yet state that communities could perhaps be considered persons and hence be right-holders, somewhat evades the difficulty. Ronald Garet sums it up well by saying that "the idea of group-personhood glimpses but then buries under the avalanche of allegory." [8]

In an attempt to sort out different kinds of community rights, Will Kymlicka proposes to distinguish between group rights and special rights. On the one hand, group rights involve the rights of groups against their own members, for example when in the name of group solidarity internal dissent is silenced. Special rights, on the other hand, do not refer to intra-group relations, but to inter-group relations: the right of a particular community against the larger society. If group rights affirm the priority of the community over the individual, special rights affirm the special status of a community within the larger state. According to Kymlicka, what is relevant in Canada—and what is justifiable—are special rights, not group rights: "Most such rights in this country concern not the primacy of communities over individuals. Rather, they are based upon the idea that justice between communities requires that the members of different groups be accorded different rights." [9] Although the distinction is analytically useful, we cannot always draw a clear line between the two types of rights. Communities that claim special status often do so because of their vulnerability to forces that do not recognize borders, forces that cut across the intra-group/inter-group distinction. As we shall see, the obstacles to the promotion of language in French Canada are not found so much in federalism, but in liberalism. Granting Québec a special status in part aims at allowing it to place restrictions on its members on the grounds that language is a most fundamental communal good to be protected. Thus special status would not only modify Québec's relationship with other federal partners, but with its own citizens as well.

To be sure, there is no easy way of justifying community rights. Perhaps part of the problem is that we forget how most of our individual rights are in some respects community rights. After all, even traditional civil rights are only intelligible in the context of a community, in this case the liberal community. They are valuable to us because they secure goods that are central to our well-being, but goods that we associate with our membership in the liberal community. On the distinction between individual rights and collective rights, Jean-Bernard Marie's comment deserves attention:

> [T]he central subject of human rights as embodied in the basic international texts is still quite definitely the irreducible human person. We are not speaking, however, of the solitary, isolated individual, but of an essentially "relating" and predominantly social being, who is always to be found in a group or community situation. And while it may be possible to speak of "individual rights", it is only because of the "individuality" of the subject of human rights and not because those rights can be conceived as restricted to an imaginary vacuum, as it were, in which the individual evolves in splendid isolation. Strictly speaking, "individual" rights do not exist in the sphere of human rights any more than do "collective" rights, or rather, all rights are individual because held by individuals and all are collective by the process of their recognition, their mode of exercise and their means of protection. [10]

To that extent, attempting to draw a neat division between the two categories of rights can be misleading.

Community rights, in the end, appear to be the special rights we claim as members of a particular community. What we think of as individual rights are those that are usually claimed as members of a liberal society, without any reference to membership in a particular linguistic or ethnic community. One's communal ties should have no bearing on the right against arbitrary detention. This is an individual right held by all of us as citizens of a liberal polity. But one's status does have bearing on special hunting and fishing rights in Canada since they can only be held by people as members of given aboriginal communities. The Aboriginal who claims the right to not being arbitrarily detained is not making the claim as an Aboriginal, but as a member of liberal society. But that same Aboriginal who claims special hunting rights is claiming a good which is central to Aboriginal membership and identity.

By extension we can expect such community rights to differ from other rights in the nature of the good which is claimed. That is not to say that communal goods necessarily give rise to community rights, since many shared goods entail rights which are not understood as being collective. Freedom of association, for example, is a good that cannot be exercised or enjoyed alone. Still I have an individual right to freedom of association: the right is bestowed on me, not on the collectivity of individuals who wish to associate. That a good is necessarily shared should not mean that a single individual cannot claim a right to it.

Moreover, having a critical mass of individuals who claim a particular good gives force to the claim, but this is not characteristic of communal goods only. Individual rights too are more easily enforceable when they are claimed by an important number of claimants. To put it differently, community rights is not what Michael McDonald calls a class action concept, where "the group as a right-holder serves as a convenient device for advancing the multiple discrete and severable interests of similarly situated individuals".[11] Rather, the idea is that there are communal goods which are central to the definition of community membership and identity, and which are usually claimed by individuals as community members.

What is involved in community rights are the communal goods of community members. I think this more clearly corresponds to what we really mean when we speak of community rights. Still, these convoluted distinctions show just how blurred the line is between individual and community rights. In the end, all our rights are claimed as community members if we think of liberalism as also reflecting a conception of community. The difference is whether a right is rooted in liberal community or rooted in our belonging in a particular community of identity.

Many will object that true rights are universal, that by definition there can be no "special" rights. Universality would command that any right bestowed on one community be bestowed on all other communities; since this makes little sense, how can special community rights be anything more than claims to special privilege? Besides, to give these special rights equal recognition, side by side with our common individual rights, is to undermine the latter by empowering communities against their members. It is a powerful objection, but one which perhaps misses the point. What we usually refer to as universal moral rights are quite often the rights that we associate with liberal ideology. [12] The fact that claims about the universality of welfare rights are sometimes mocked upon attests to this. Welfare rights, after all, do not have deep roots in liberal ideology. Liberalism and universality are so intimately tied in the dominant ideology that things not liberal could not be universal, and things not universal are illiberal. Invoking supposedly universal entitlements against claims made by members of vulnerable communities unfortunately too often conceals hegemonic projects. What we must remember, then, is that rights-discourse is construed in a liberal framework, so that rights make sense to us against a certain background understanding of what interests are meant to be protected. To put it differently, systems of rights, such as the one found in Canada, presuppose values that resonate in the liberal community. Rights are not abstract entitlements of cryptic origins, but moral relations between citizens of a particular polity. Alleged universal claims, to put it differently, are not over and above liberal society, floating in a timeless realm of morality, but very much a part of it. Rights are a language we give ourselves as citizens, but citizens of a particular community.

Whether individual or communal, rights are a way of expressing those claims to human goods that are most urgent. Many of these basic goods are abstract—dignity, autonomy, integrity, identity. Not only do each of these goods engender derivatives that take a concrete shape according to circumstances, time and place, but the moral arguments for claiming them as rights find niches in different ideologies. [13] Liberalism articulates for us a set of values and beliefs that we cherish, most notably through individual rights-discourse. But as Leslie Green notes, these correspond to our individuated interests, such as liberty and security, and surely do not encompass all that is worthwhile.[14] The importance of preserving the conditions of our identity also needs to find a place in rights-discourse.

The notorious conflict between individual rights and collective rights takes on a different shade, for it is not the reflection of a collision between the individual and the community, but of a tension among competing claims to goods that equally contribute to our well-being. Granted this does not make rights-talk any more harmonious, since we are nevertheless talking about a collision between these different kinds of rights, not about their reconciliation. I am suspicious of attempts at reconciliation when they hope to show that community rights are not a threat after all. These often have the effect of evacuating conflict by the skillful use of philosophical argument. Much of the literature favourable to community rights is along those lines. What we have instead is a real tension between different claims derived from different substantive values, yet one that can be better managed with an improved understanding of the value of communal goods and membership.

But having said all of that, there is something unappealing to the idea that all moral requirements ought to take the form of rights. Translating so indeterminate a notion as the preservation of a communal identity into the language of community rights risks saturating rights-discourse to the point where it loses force and credibility. That would do little good to those urgent claims that still need to be resolved. Jeremy Waldron points out how abusing rights-discourse leads to "head-on confrontation between rival claims made in language which—no matter what cautions are offered by the prudent philosopher—continues to evince an air of stridency, absolutism and the repudiation of compromise."[15] Not all conflicts between interests, he argues, should be understood as conflicts over rights, for some interests cannot be adequately expressed in terms of rights or else lack the sense of urgency that rights should convey. He goes on to say that "the language of moral rights is a special currency whose value should be jealously protected and not debased by being used as a vehicle for just any interest or preferences".[16]

Faced with these doubts about the use of rights to express communal claims, it is tempting to reserve the language of rights for those claims that fall under the rubric of more traditional (liberal) individual rights. This would also have the advantage of facilitating the adjudication of inevitable clashes between competing claims. The promotion of communities and communal goods could consist instead in the judiciable task of setting reasonable limits to the exercise of traditional individual rights, thus indirectly accounting for the value of non-individualized goods. [17] This normative discourse, the argument goes, could express collective claims without creating a new category of rights and without risking a constitutional overload.

However, the objection that rights are best reserved to express individualized claims need not exclude collective claims. I think part of the resistance stems from an understanding of rights as possessive entitlements. Joel Feinberg writes that "[r]ights are themselves property, things we own, and from which we may not even temporarily be dispossessed". [18] If we conceive rights simply as what is "mine" and "yours", then it is easy to see how the addition of community rights might damage what is left of our social fabric and kill any hope of achieving solidarity in an already dislocated world. [19] This kind of rhetoric assumes a zero-sum game, notes Staughton Lynd, "which pictures us as separated owners of our respective bundles of rights". [20]

But rights denote foremost a moral relation between us. It is a relation that imposes duties when an appeal to the goodwill or moral concern of the majority offers few guarantees. Rights allow us to discern amongst moral considerations those that have an urgency, that matter most, and hence that justify the correlative duties. Our sense of what justice and human dignity require can be translated into a set of rights which have moral weight in the face of various other considerations. Rights give us grounds for imposing constraints on other people's actions that would treat us as means to some end, however appealing the end might be. We value rights because, as Colin Wringe writes, we see ourselves "as beings whose wishes may not be lightly set aside, however great the benefit to be derived from so doing". [21] Rights discourse is therefore a powerful device to claim the goods that are central to our autonomy *and* to our identity. Not using rights-talk to express our most fundamental moral claims to community relegates them to a subordinate position where they can be easily "trumped" (to borrow Ronald Dworkin's term) by established rights. But what is more, rights can in fact serve to articulate conflict and foster a deeper solidarity between otherwise competing elements of society. Christine Sypnowich makes an interesting point in that regard:

> Democratic debate does not occur in a homogeneous community; a citizenry which values agreement above all else would make poor participants in a democracy. Because rights can articulate and resolve individual differences, rights can serve democratic institutions. Indeed, it could be argued that even the phenomenon of solidarity depends on the articulation of difference. Solidarity emerges when discrete individuals understand that they share wider concerns. By articulating and resolving differences between individuals and individuals and society, rights therefore can have a valuable role to play in even the most harmonious of communities. [22]

Even in disharmonious communities, I would add, rights provide us with the necessary moral language to express our disagreements, cast them against each other and, if not resolve our differences, to at least give them a vocabulary.

Of all the meanings that can be given to community rights, we can defend a version that remains compatible with our understanding of what rights are all about in the first place. Most people who believe in community fortunately avoid the temptation of invoking obscure entitlements that would only make sense if communities were living entities. Their inclination (and mine) is to reject the strong version of collective rights, namely that communities command respect as moral agents in the same way that individuals do. In our mainstream ideology, communities cannot be right-holders because they are not moral agents, that is, they do not have an inherent value making them self-originating sources of valid claims. But the problem is that liberals are too quick to reject reasonable attempts at rehabilitating collective claims into the language of rights. A weaker, yet more defensible, version can properly express claims to the protection of communal goods derived from the value of identity, and need not reach beyond the fulfilment of individual well-being. Community rights do make sense when taken as a way to voice those urgent interests that are naturally relational in the pursuit and enjoyment of a communal good. The purpose of such rights is grounded in the recognition that individuals need communal goods in order to live a worthy life. Some claims are inseparable from the particular community in which they arise, both in terms of the good being central to the community's life and of the claimant being a community member who values the good. Objections fall short when community rights are viewed this way. It then becomes clear that the alleged conflict between the individual and the community in fact reveals an inevitable tension among valid moral claims themselves, but claims that all aim at enhancing individual well-being. The question is whether language can be considered a good that is fundamental enough to be the subject-matter of rights. We must therefore ask how language relates to identity.

Notes

1. See Virginia McDonald, "A Liberal Democratic Response to the Canadian Crisis", in *Philosophers Look at Canadian Confederation*, ed. Stanley G. French (Montreal: The Canadian Philosophical Association, 1979), 328-329.

2. Michael Hartney, "Some Confusions Concerning Collective Rights", *The Canadian Journal of Law and Jurisprudence* 4, no. 2 (July 1991): 297.

3. See Michael McDonald's point on this issue in "The Rights of People and the Rights of a People", in *Philosophers Look at Canadian Confederation*, 336.

4. This is Joseph Raz's approach in "Right-based Morality", in *Theories of Rights*, ed. Jeremy Waldron (Oxford: Oxford University Press, 1984), 194-195. It is also Lesley Jacobs' approach in "Bridging the Gap Between Individual and Collective Rights With the Idea of Integrity", *The Canadian Journal of Law and Jurisprudence* 4, no. 2 (July 1991): 384.

5. Jacobs follows this approach in "Bridging the Gap Between Individual and Collective Rights With the Idea of Integrity", 384.

6. Jeremy Waldron, "Rights, Public Choice and Communal Goods", 6-7.

7. Vernon Van Dyke, "Collective Entities and Moral Rights: Problems in Liberal-Democratic Thought", *Journal of Politics* 44, no. 1 (February 1982): 22.

8. Garet, "Communality and Existence: The Rights of Groups", 1039.

9. Will Kymlicka, "Individual and Community Rights", in *Group Rights*, ed. Judith Baker (Toronto: University of Toronto Press, 1994), 28.

10. Jean-Bernard Marie, "Relations Between Peoples' Rights and Human Rights: Semantic and Methodological Distinctions", *Human Rights Law Journal* 7, no. 2-4 (1986): 199; Also see Hector Gros Espiell, "The Right of Development as a Human Right", *Texas International Law Journal* 16, no. 2 (Spring 1981): 194-195.

11. McDonald, "Should Communities Have Rights? Reflections on Liberal Individualism", 218.

12. See for example Hartney, "Some Confusions Concerning Collective Rights", 311. Following W. S. Tarnopolsky, he speaks of universal rights we all have in virtue of being humans, and collective rights some of us have in virtue of belonging to a particular group. It is a distinction which I had also subscribed to in "Making Sense of Law 101 in the Age of the Charter", *Québec Studies* 17 (Winter 1994), but with which I now feel less comfortable. I prefer to see those alleged universal rights as rights grounded in liberal society.

13. For an interesting perspective on abstract and derivative rights, see Jacobs, "Bridging the Gap Between Individual and Collective Rights With the Idea of Integrity", 381-382.

14. Leslie Green, "Two Views of Collective Rights", *The Canadian Journal of Law and Jurisprudence* 4, no. 2 (July 1991): 317.

15. Waldron, "Rights, Public Choice and Communal Goods", 2.

16. Waldron, "Rights, Public Choice and Communal Goods", 4.

17. See McDonald, "Should Communities Have Rights? Reflections on Liberal Individualism", 228.

18. Feinberg, *Rights, Justice, and the Bounds of Liberty*, 75.

19. On this issue see Kenneth L. Schmitz, "Is Liberalism Good Enough?", in *Liberalism and the Good*, ed. R. Bruce Gouglas, Gerald M. Mara, and Henry S. Richardson (New York: Routledge, 1990), 99.

20. Staughton Lynd, "Communal Rights", *Texas Law Review* 62, no. 8 (May 1984): 1419.

21. Wringe, *Children's Rights: A Philosophical Study*, 36.

22.   Christine Sypnowich, "Rights, Community and the Charter", *British Journal of Canadian Studies* 6, no. 1 (1991): 46-47.

4

The Language-Identity Link

Trying to discern the importance of language in people's lives inevitably leads to the deeper problem of identity. If we believe in the value of identity to human flourishing, we can articulate strong reasons for language to be considered a fundamental communal good and, as it will become clear, for saying that it should give rise to rights. To do so, we must interpret how language relates to identity. One difficulty lies in the fact there are many different manifestations of these ties, and those selected here, although they bear upon particular circumstances, may not enable us to reach an overall judgment. My aim here is to identify answers that can be given to this question: Why is language so important?

While it is somewhat of a truism to state that language can influence the shaping of identity, it remains useful to see more precisely what meanings can be given to this assertion. We must put into different perspectives the various claims about the relationship between language and identity. In particular, we must consider how language plays on perceptions of who we think we are. Also, at the basis of the language-identity link is the contentious assertion that language patterns impose a specific structuring of reality and determine the way we look at the world. This is a difficult question, but it remains relevant to sketch its main elements. Moreover, the problem of translation is sometimes invoked as an additional reason for identifying mainly with one's language; we shall see if there is evidence to support this claim. Finally, the question of language in the context of nationalism is of particular interest here and merits some attention, for it often hinges on the notion of national identity.

Of course, to say that the faculty of language is a good does not require much demonstration. After all, language is a universal method of communication, the primary medium used to express thoughts, so it can easily be imagined what life would be without it. The difficulty resides elsewhere: given that language in general is a good, can we say that one's *own* language is also a good?

Part of the answer can be found in the relation between language and ethnic identity. The difficulty in examining this relationship, however, stems from the vagueness involved in the concept of ethnicity. Consider how Joshua Fishman describes it:

> Ethnicity is rightly understood as an aspect of a collectivity's self-recognition as well as an aspect of its recognition in the eyes of outsiders. ... [I]t is an avenue whereby individuals are linked to society, i. e. to social norms and to social values. Like them, ethnicity represents an avenue whereby understandings of the "world at large" are arrived at, that is to say, through ethnicity ordinary individuals are not only linked to collectivities—and social integration is attained thereby—but to notions of "life", "society" and "the world" as well. [1]

Ethnicity, then, is a powerful mediator for shared values and understandings. Some aspects of ethnicity are inherited (what Fishman calls paternity) while other aspects are acquired (what he calls patrimony). Paternity, in the sense of biological origins, often appears as the central dimension of ethnicity since it defines one's descent-related existence. Patrimony, on the other hand, is acquired behaviour. Paternity is a state of being, whereas patrimony is behavioural, or, as Fishman puts it, "[p]aternity defines those who inherit a heritage", while "[p]atrimony is the bulk of that heritage".[2] Significantly, there is much subjectivity in the meanings one attaches to one's ethnicity, whether acquired or inherited and, we might add, whether real or imaginary.

Ethnicity can denote many different features: objective biological origins, cultural artefacts, subjective perceptions about our belonging. The notion of ethnicity abounds in the literature on language, and its meaning remains diffuse.[3] Still, it is pertinent to ask how language influences perceptions of ourselves and of what group we think we belong to. We can then capture better the relation between identity and language, as well as the problem of ethnicity which interfaces in complex ways between the two. I shall first examine two sets of arguments: those that suggest a weak link between language and identity, and those that support the claim about language being central to identity.

After having studied perceptions of identity in the face of language change, Carol Eastman has come to the conclusion that there is no necessary link between language and identity. She notes that "when we stop using the language of our ethnic group, only the language use aspect of our ethnic identity changes; the primordial sense of who we are and what group we think we belong to for the remainder remains intact". [4] For example, a French person living in New York may stop using the French language and even lose the ability to speak it, but that person remains French until all factors of that identity change—namely, until his perception of ancestry changes. As she writes: "If the group can get what it needs to maintain itself using its associated language it will. If it can get what it needs wearing ethnic dress it will. However, necessary changes in dress and language use need not change group identity".[5] Thus according to Eastman, language change and changes in identity are two separate processes. Even when the surface behavioural aspects (*speaking* French) have disappeared or are no longer used, the primordial identity (*being* French) may remain over a long period of time: "Hence we don't have to speak French to act French and believe we are French".[6] In sum, "we change the language we know and use without changing our ethnic primordial identity...".[7] There would therefore be surface behavioural aspects of ethnic identity, more easily disposable, and primordial aspects of ethnic identity, more durable. Language would be a surface marker of identity that can be altered without fundamental changes to the way we perceive ourselves, or, more precisely, language shift would only affect the language use aspect of our identity, which Eastman sees as a "very low level of manifestation of our cultural belief system".[8] This is significant, for if linguistic assimilation need not mean total assimilation but only loss of a surface marker of identity, then policies aiming at protecting a given language may lose their relative urgency. As Eastman admits, "there is no need to worry about preserving ethnic identity, so long as the only change being made is in what language we use".[9] The implications of this can be far-reaching in the context of language planning in multilingual societies, for preserving primordial identities, it would seem, does not require preserving languages. So there would appear to be no necessary connection between the language we speak and who we think we are.

Another indication that identity and language might be linked only contingently is found in the integration of immigrants. Looking at this question in the United States, John Edwards observed that some markers of identity (such as a particular way of dressing) are discarded while others (such as religious practices) are preserved. His observations also indicate that immigrants make voluntary efforts to speak English, which suggests a desire to avoid segregation from mainstream life, or the need to assure upward mobility.[10] This shows that some markers of identity (in this case a particular way of dressing, and even the mother tongue) may not be primordial, and thus can be partly discarded without suffering any true loss of identity. Leaving one's language at home in exchange for public acceptance indeed may not be a bad trade off. Other markers of identity, however, may not be as superficial (in this example religious observance), and thus do not sit well with policies of integration.

What Eastman and Edwards' observations suggest is that language has no fixed rank within the order of what constitutes a primordial factor of identity and what constitutes a surface marker of identity. So the notion that language is *necessarily* related to our identity in a primordial sense is not substantiated. Still, this should not allure us to conclude that language can *never* be a constitutive factor of our primordial identity. For many, language is a key factor of identity, an "identification badge", as Muriel Saville-Troike puts it: "Having a shared culture, having a native name with which members identify, having a social network for contact, and having common folklore or history are all largely dependent on having a common mode of communication."[11] In a similar vein, Sélim Abou explains how language mediates between all aspects of culture; by giving them a name, a meaning, and a value, language symbolizes culture in its totality.[12] Similarly, as Fishman suggests, since language carries, records, and calls forth other factors of identity (dress, food, worship), it is likely to be singled out as the main marker of identity.[13] By extension, real or perceived threats to one's language can be felt as threats to one's distinct existence.

There are numerous cases of communities whose prime marker of identity is their traditional language. This is sometimes manifest in the language itself. For example, Bud Khleif explains that the Welsh word *Iaith* originally meant both community and language; the word to designate a foreigner is *Anghyfiaith*, meaning "not of the same language", while the word to designate compatriot is *Cyfiaith*, meaning "of the same language".[14] Or consider the case of the Basques. Christopher Cobb observes that the term *Euskalherria* designates the region where *Euskera* (the Basque language) is spoken, *euskaldunes* those who speak Basque and *erdeldunes* those who speak other languages such as Castilian or French.[15] These various words link language with culture, history, and other artefacts in such a way that language acquires highly symbolic properties in the definition of "who belongs". But as argued above, these links remain contingent and circumstantial.

The importance of language in defining identity also varies in degree and in kind. For instance, the majority/minority variable influences perceptions of self and others. Being conscious of boundaries between one's smaller linguistic group and society at large may reinforce linguistic identity.[16] Individuals may have a stronger linguistic identity when their minority status contrasts with the dominant language. Jean Laponce argues that being in a vulnerable position, members of a linguistic minority tend to shelter their weakness in a clearly defined identity that serves as a kind of protective cage. When language marks the separation between a vulnerable community and dominant society, the individual in a minority position will be particularly conscious of his language since it delimits his range of action.[17] Here we see that language acquires the property to establish boundaries that serve to differentiate and protect oneself from the majority. Language serves to maintain boundaries that mark off one community from another, or, to put it differently, that determine identity insofar as identity is rooted in social and even spatial boundaries. As Khleif writes, "[i]f boundaries define belonging, if identity itself is anchored in boundaries, then a decreasing emphasis on, or a blurring of, boundaries would be regarded as a threat to group existence...".[18]

Furthermore, the kinds of attachments people have to language vary. As Eastman suggests, there are instrumental attachments to language, for instance when a group learns the language that opens the doors to a better life. Problems sometimes arise when a given community cannot use its own language for instrumental purposes, perhaps because it lacks prestige, or else because it is only spoken by a small minority. This type of situation can be perceived as an attack on the very existence of the speech community in which people have a sentimental attachment to their language. [19]

The language-identity link, it would seem, cannot be understood in isolation from other factors of identity and from the specific conditions in which it is experienced. Indeed, the relationship between language and identity is far from being a static one because different communities give different meanings to the role of language depending on their relations with other groups, their stage of development, or simply the presence of other, stronger factors of identity.[20] The relation between language and identity is contingent upon subjective factors and particular circumstances. The language we speak can be crucial to our identity if we define ourselves by it, or it can be a superficial marker of our identity, one that can be abandoned without any real loss of the sense of who we are. "In other words", writes Alan Anderson, "if an ethnic group has tended to emphasize maintenance of its own traditional language, loss of that language will be equated largely with loss of group identity".[21] Conversely, it is possible for a group to lose its distinctive language without losing its identity. Therefore, we should not fall prey to the claim that language is necessarily the primary feature of identity, *nor* should we subscribe to the view that language is always a disposable marker of collective identity. The language-identity interface is far too variable to posit a definitive conceptual scheme, thus one must be cautious in examining the different roles that language carries in different communities.

Also of interest to sociolinguists is the relationship between language and thought, more specifically, the question of how language influences world outlooks. The question centres on whether the structure of a given language can structure perceptions of reality itself, and thus whether language has a constitutive role in the building of cognition. In other words, content would be dependent upon linguistic form so that a diversity of languages would necessarily imply a diversity of contents. We can take notice of two different views: on the one hand, linguistic determinism, which states that a given language determines the thought of those who speak it, and on the other hand, a set of more moderate claims about the influences of language on thought. [22]

Many of the theories that espouse some form of linguistic determinism are based on the so-called Sapir-Whorf thesis, after Edward Sapir and Benjamin Lee Whorf. According to Paul Ghils, this thesis states that the structure of a given language imposes a certain perception of the world. The belief that languages "are dissimilar because they refer to dissimilar facts", he explains, is challenged by the idea that "facts are dissimilar for speakers whose linguistic background gives a dissimilar formulation of them". [23] The realm of phenomena appears to us in a flux of impressions which are "organized by the system of concepts embodied in the patterns of our language". [24] Sapir's point was that the language a people speaks shapes its universe because its experience is organized by language, and consequently each language represents a distinct world view. Sapir did consider language as a cultural product, but he argued that language, as a social product, also influences the way a speech community conceives reality. Language is conditioned by and is the product of experience, but it also shapes this experience because its built-in categories and values are projected into the world of phenomena. In other words, explains Ghils, there is a dialectical relation between language as a "stock of experience" and language as a "creative system". Following Sapir, though more radically, Whorf argued that the formulation of ideas is not independent from the language being used, for a given language cuts up experience according to its grammar structure, categories, and types. Therefore there would be no universal logic, but rather different systems for screening impressions and organizing concepts.

In short, the implication of the Sapir-Whorf hypothesis is that people speaking different languages may have different cultural outlooks even if they share the same environment since the particular structure of each language imposes a specific structuring of reality. Posing such an intimate relationship between language and world views is not without consequence to the question of identity. For if the way we look at the world and at ourselves is determined in part by the language we speak, then the preservation of our way of life and of our identity requires (at the least) protecting the language we speak. The link between language and identity would therefore be an objective and necessary one. "Extending this thought", writes Eastman, "becoming a speaker of a different language would change a person's self-identity".[25]

The main question, then, looks like this: given the reasonable assumption that one's thought is closely related to the formation of one's identity, to what extent can we say that language, by virtue of having an influence on thought, shapes identity? If we took the language determinist view, it would follow that language is a primary and objective factor of identity.

Nothing essential for our purposes depends upon the solving of this difficult question. It should be noted, however, that the consensus which has emerged from most recent studies points to the lack of evidence to support the language determinism thesis in full. There is no strong evidence to assume a close relationship between linguistic forms and cultural characteristics, which leads many to conclude that the language people speak does not bind them to a particular world view. [26] It should also be stressed that theories concurrent with the language determinist view tend to compare language systems that are significantly different, e. g. European languages versus American Indian languages. It is argued that these two language families do not share the same basic characteristics considering they have dissimilar modes of classification of events and dissimilar categories of time and space. [27] Thus it is difficult to see how the Sapir-Whorf hypothesis could be supported by comparing, say, French and English. In any case, it is worth noting the implications of the language determinism thesis on the building of cognition and hence on the formation of identity.

But whether or not ideas are determined by language, there is a different set of considerations which relates to the problem of translation. Are languages perfectly translatable? For if not, some ideas expressed in one language could not be expressed in another language. Some of the thoughts about ourselves and our environment would be, to some extent, bound to the language we speak. The subtleties in meanings and understandings could only be shared by those who speak the same language, or the same version of it. Our identity would be bound not only to our experiences, but to the language which expresses these experiences in a genuine way, without loss of meaning.

On the surface, it seems that the problem of translation is not insurmountable. As Jane Hill writes, "[w]ork on problems in intercultural communication ... shows that very different cultural patterning can be expressed in the same language ...".[28] This can be explained by looking at the resources that every language has to allow its speakers to express virtually any idea. Elaine Chaika sums up well the objection:

> So far as linguists know, all languages are mutually translatable. What can be said in one language can be said in any other—somehow. All languages are so constructed that new thoughts can be expressed in them. To be sure, it is easier to express some ideas in one language than another. This is because the vocabulary of each language develops partly according to the priorities of its culture. The objects, relationships, activities, and ideas important to the culture get coded into single words which are often highly specialized to express subtle nuances. ... In fact, although it may be difficult to express a given idea in one language rather than another, there has never been any proof that it is impossible. [29]

We must therefore mitigate the claim that languages are not truly translatable, and thus that the expression of one's experiences loses meaning through translation.

However, there is still something to be said about the problem of translation. First, even though languages can *somehow* be translated by experts in the field, it remains to be seen whether people in general have this capacity, as Edward Stewart argues:

> The capacity exists in any language to say whatever is said in any other language. What I can say in English can be said in French, Russian, Urdu, or Hindi. There are procedures of translation and back translation, and specialists exist in these areas who can demonstrate with exquisite skill that the capability of English is precisely that of Urdu or Farsi.

However, he goes on to say that

> [n]ormally a speaker does not deliver the full capability of the language on a given occasion. The speaker selects, forgets, distorts linguistic features of language capability to create a message. [30]

Assuming that most people express themselves better in one language than another, then the optimal transmission of a message—one that carries meanings about one's being and experiences—will be partly confined to that language. Some emotions and intimate meanings are not easily translatable, especially those that are identity-related, and thus require a shared understanding which only the subtleties of a common language can provide.[31]

A second reason for taking the problem of translation seriously stems from studies on bilingualism. It is suggested that unilinguals and subordinate bilinguals (those who show more proficiency in one language) equate a word learned in the second language with the word in their native tongue, rather than with the object the word refers to. For example, an English speaker would associate the newly-learned French word *livre* with the word "book", as opposed to both words being independently associated with their referents.[32] What this situation seems to imply is that the native language has a dimension which goes beyond its function as a sign since it can be intimately linked with what is being signified. This fusion of word and object suggests that one's experience of the world and of oneself (among unilinguals and subordinate bilinguals) is closely associated to one's native language. This further supports the idea that the language we speak can be part of our views of the world and of our identity.

Finally, it should also be stressed that as language is rooted in a specific reality, it contains various cultural, social, political and economic elements of this reality. To translate the language implies de-rooting it, or at least evacuating some of its content. Fishman writes how language is

> not merely a carrier of content, whether latent or manifest. Language itself is content, a referent for loyalties and animosities, an indicator of social statuses and personal relationships, a marker of situations and topics as well as of the societal goals and the larger-scale value-laden arenas of interaction that typify every speech community.[33]

Language contains a reality in itself; to transform the language is to transform the reality, or at least the image of this reality. Consider for example *joual* (a popular version of Québécois French spoken mostly in Montreal) which can be translated into standard international French, and into any other language for that matter. But the translation would not be able to fully capture the reality behind joual, that of a disadvantaged social class whose language style not only results from this disadvantaged position, but also serves to maintain it. Since the two are intimately linked, a translation would bring much distortion to this socioeconomic condition.

In view of these three remarks, we see that the problem of translation cannot be completely discarded, for our identity is to a certain extent part of the language we speak.

Another often invoked link is the one between language and nationalism, especially since many language planning efforts are guided by nationalist ideology. We know that a nation denotes an association of a wider scope and complexity than other associations. As Fishman writes, a common nationality expresses "a more advanced degree and inclusive scope or scale of effective organization and of elaborated beliefs, values, and behaviours than those that obtain in the case of ethnic groups per se".[34] Ernest Renan defined the nation in more subjective terms: "Avoir des gloires communes dans le passé, une volonté commune dans le présent; avoir fait de grandes choses ensemble; vouloir en faire encore. Voilà les conditions essentielles pour être un peuple". [Having common glories in the past, a common will in the present; having done great things together; wanting to do more. These are the essential conditions to be a people.][35] This kind of "everyday plebiscite" is compatible with many different circumstances. Here there appears to be no single objective criterion that defines what a nation is. The will of the people is sufficient. Yet various shared features, alone or in combination, often unite people: culture, religion, ethnicity, history, ideology, and, of course, language. It would be misleading to discard these objective features as conditions for nationhood. The will of the people may be essential for nationhood, but this subjective factor often arises because of conditions such as a common language, ethnicity, or religion.[36]

More important is the fact that nationality is not the same as citizenship, which denotes a constitutional status comprising rights and duties attached to state membership. In this sense, state and nation are different. Nationalism, then, is the ideological framework in which are organized the attempts of a nationality to pursue or maintain sovereignty of the nation. It wishes to see the nation gain power over the public dimension of its existence, by seeking congruity with its existing citizenship, or else by calling for the creation of a redefined citizenship altogether. Not surprisingly, nationalism involves demands that challenge the fundamental structure of the state's constitution, especially when   political independence is sought by a distinct nationality as a way of reconfigurating its citizenship.

Nationalism and communal identification are not unrelated. Fishman writes that nationalism may seek to "derive unifying and energizing power from widely held images of the past in order to overcome a quite modern kind of fragmentation and loss of identity". [37] In that sense nationalism can be a response to the loss of traditional markers of identity by providing a redefinition of community-shared purposes. Likewise Charles Taylor argues that nationalism is a modern form of communal identification where the members of a nation find a community of interests and feelings that goes beyond the interdependence involved in the production and exchange of commodities. The nation, he suggests, can be central to its members because through it they have access to their identity and to a "horizon of meaning". This explains why the nationalist line emphasizes the need for the nation to express itself, to achieve goals of its own, and to be recognized as having a distinct experience. [38]

What of the language-nationalism link? Some have held the view that a national language is the expression of the nation's soul, that it is the guardian of an authenticity inherited from glorious ancestors and to be handed down to future generations. [39] Somewhat less romantically, we all know that a common language is not a necessary criterion for nationhood. But as Fishman points out, there is still a need to explain why language is sometimes believed to have a central role in nationalism and why some modern nationalist movements have taken the linguistic line. [40]

To be sure, language can serve nationalist ideology in the confrontation with the wider state or with other states. The Catalan language, for example, became the motor of the nationalist movement:

> The fact that [Catalan] had been the sole language and at times officially recognized interwove the political movements for greater recognition of Catalonia as a distinct cultural region (and one capable of managing its own affairs) with attempts to make Catalan into the official language for the area, if not actually the sole recognized form of communication. [41]

The same could be said of Galician nationalist ideology[42] and, as I will discuss in further chapters, of French-Canadian and Québécois nationalisms. The point is that there are cases where nationalist ideology and the national language go hand in hand because people identify themselves and their nationhood with the language they speak, or else because nationalist leaders use language as a tool to regenerate the nation.

We see that nationalism is about power and control by a nationality over the public sphere, and that these relations of power are sometimes embodied in language issues. In that regard, Taylor's argument is inspiring. If it is through community that we have access to a horizon of meaning, to our identity, and to a network of common understandings, then it is essential for us that our language be preserved. The national language (in the sense of both speech and outlook) needs to gain expressive power by being used in various sectors of life, namely the economy, the arts, the government, management, and technology. But more importantly, for the nation to express itself, it must achieve things of its own: "If the important realizations are brought about by other peoples, then the language of public life, of economic-management, of technology, etc., will almost inevitably be a foreign one".[43] If this be the case, and given the premise that we define ourselves through collective eyes, then members of the said nation may depreciate themselves and lose their self-respect as they depreciate their language for its lack of achievements and power. This would explain, he continues, why the nationalist position will be to value that language/culture so that members will value themselves and regain their self-respect. It will also involve gaining some form of recognition, for it is difficult for anyone to maintain an identity if the conditions for that identity are denied by others. Taylor's argument illustrates well how language and identity relate to notions of power and control over the public sphere.

In sum, the language-nationalism link is also a contingent one. A nation's historical circumstances will dictate its importance, if any. Still there are cases where language and identity do meet in nationalism because nationalist ideology offers the possibility to exercise power over the nation's constitutive identity, over its language.

So why is language important? In general, the answers revolve around the observation that one's language contributes to giving a concrete shape to one's distinctness as a person, while at the same time providing a matrix for communal identification. That is why the significance of language as either a marker or a constitutive factor of identity should not be overlooked. Though there is no necessary relation between language and identity, we cannot discard the fact there are individuals and communities who find in language the source of their distinctness. Moreover, language is a social product and plays a role (however limited) in the building of cognition. This suggests that language is more than a means of communication for, it would seem to a certain extent, it also contributes to shaping our understanding of the world. We must also keep in mind that however surmountable the problem of translation is for sociolinguists, it remains a real difficulty for most of us. Our identity, therefore, remains bound not only to our experiences, but also to the language which best expresses these. Evoking some of the ties between language and nationalist ideology further shows how some modern nationalisms are founded on a claim to a distinct language which marks or even constitutes the distinctness of the nation.

In short, language gives access to, and is one of the creative forces of, shared meanings and understandings, which together contribute to define identity. This dynamic can find a concrete form in nationalist ideology which offers solutions to provide the national language with expressive power over the public sphere. This puts into perspective some of the presumed links between language and identity. If a conclusion can be drawn, it is that language situations are the result of particular histories and circumstances, so that it remains a venture to generalize how language relates to identity. Each case warrants special attention to determine the nature of the relationship between language and identity. There is little doubt, however, that language can encompass more than a means of communication, and that language community can give us access to the cultural material that defines our identity and that shapes our ideas about fulfillment. On these grounds we can articulate the reasons for saying that language, as a communal good central to our identity, might give rise to rights.

To sum up Part I, there is a version of liberalism which occupies too much room in Canada's political culture. It is a version that cannot fully recognize those deep attachments to communities of identity, such as language communities. The problem has its source in an understanding of such attachments as being secondary in our moral deliberations about the principles of justice that ought to regulate basic institutions. The end-product is a discourse about rights whose built-in categories tend to exclude those valid claims to communal goods. I, like many others, think this version is mistaken. There is another way to construe liberal society so that those goods that are important not only to our autonomy but to our identity as well be given proper consideration. Community rights allow us to do just that. They improve our moral relations through a mutual respect of communal ties that constitute the substance of who we are.

Notes

1.   Joshua A. Fishman, *Language and Ethnicity in Minority Sociolinguistic Perspective* (Philadelphia: Multilingual Matters Ltd, 1989), 24.

2.   Fishman, *Language and Ethnicity in Minority Sociolinguistic Perspective*, 27-29.

3.   Michael Keating, for example, argues that the problem with the concept of ethnicity is that it "is not defined independently of the phenomenon which it is supposed to explain". He suggests it would make more sense "to talk simply of identity". See his *State and Regionalism: Territorial Politics and the European State* (London: Harvester Wheatsheaf, 1988), 15-16.

4.   Carol Eastman, "Language, Ethnic Identity and Change", in *Linguistic Minorities, Policies and Pluralism*, ed. John Edwards (London: Academic Press, 1984), 261.

5.   Eastman, "Language, Ethnic Identity and Change", 263.

6.   Eastman, "Language, Ethnic Identity and Change", 270.

7. Eastman, "Language, Ethnic Identity and Change", 270.

8. Eastman, "Language, Ethnic Identity and Change", 275.

9. Eastman, "Language, Ethnic Identity and Change", 275.

10. John Edwards, "Language, Diversity and Identity", in *Linguistic Minorities, Policies and Pluralism*, ed. John Edwards (London: Academic Press, 1984), 281, 292-293.

11. Muriel Saville-Troike, *The Ethnography of Communication* (Oxford: Basil Blackwell, 1989), 20.

12. Sélim Abou, "Éléments pour une théorie générale de l'aménagement linguistique", *Actes du Colloque international sur l'aménagement linguistique*, ed. Lorne Laforge (Québec: Les Presses de l'Université Laval, 1987), 7.

13. Fishman, *Language and Ethnicity in Minority Sociolinguistic Perspective*, 31-33.

14. Bud B. Khleif, "Insiders, Outsiders, and Renegades: Towards a Classification of Ethnolinguistic Labels", in *Language and Ethnic Relations*, ed. Howard Giles and Bernard Saint-Jacques (Oxford: Pergamon Press, 1979), 160.

15. Christopher H. Cobb, "Basque Language Teaching: From Clandestinity to Official Policy", *Journal of Area Studies* 11 (Spring 1985): 7.

16. Fishman, *Language and Ethnicity in Minority Sociolinguistic Perspective*, 33.

17. Jean Laponce, *Langue et territoire* (Québec: Les Presses de l'Université Laval, 1984), 40-41.

18. Khleif, "Insiders, Outsiders, and Renegades: Towards a Classification of Ethnolinguistic Labels", 159.

19. Carol Eastman, *Language Planning* (San Francisco: Chandler and Sharp, 1983), 34-35.

20. Jeffrey A. Ross, "Language and the Mobilization of Ethnic Identity", *Language and Ethnic Relations*, ed. Howard Giles and Bernard Saint-Jacques (Oxford: Pergamon Press, 1979), 4.

21. Alan B. Anderson, "The Survival of Ethnolinguistic Minorities: Canadian and Comparative Research", in *Language and Ethnic Relations*, 68.

22. For a description of these two views, see Eastman, *Language Planning*, 75-76.

23. Paul Ghils, *Language and Thought* (New York: Vantage Press, 1980), 1.

24.   Ghils, *Language and Thought*, 1.

25.   Eastman, *Language Planning*, 47.

26.   See for example Ronald Wardhaugh, *The Contexts of Language* (Rowley: Newburry, 1976), 74.

27.   See Ghils, *Language and Thought*, 7.

28.   Jane H. Hill, "Language, Culture, and World View", in *Language: The Sociocultural Context*, Linguistics: The Cambridge Survey, vol. 4, ed. Frederick J. Newmeyer (Cambridge: Cambridge University Press, 1988), 16.

29.   Elaine Chaika, *Language: The Social Mirror* (Rowley: Newburry House, 1982), 195.

30.   Edward C. Stewart, "Talking Culture: Language in the Function of Communication", in *The First Delaware Symposium on Language Studies*, ed. Robert J. DiPietro et al. (Newark: University of Delaware Press, 1983), 24.

31.   See Donald M. Taylor and Howard Giles, "At the Crossroads of Research into Language and Ethnic Relations", in *Language and Ethnic Relations*, 232.

32.   On this question, see Jay Kettle-Williams, "On Bilingualism", *Journal of Area Studies* 11 (Spring 1985): 5.

33.   Joshua Fishman, *The Sociology of Language* (Rowley: Newburry Publishers, 1972), 4.

34.   Fishman, *Language and Ethnicity in Minority Sociolinguistic Perspective*, 107.

35.   Ernest Renan, quoted by Desmond Morton, "Divided Loyalties? Divided Country?", in *Belonging: The Meaning and Future of Canadian Citizenship*, ed. William Kaplan (Montreal and Kingston: McGill-Queen's University Press, 1993), 53. My translation.

36.   Carl Friedrich, "The Politics of Language and Corporate Federalism", *Les États multilingues: problèmes et solutions*. ed. Jean-Guy Savard and Richard Vigneault (Québec: Les Presses de l'Université Laval, 1975), 228, 231.

37.   Fishman, *Language and Ethnicity in Minority Sociolinguistic Perspective*, 113-114.

38.   Charles Taylor, "Why Do Nations Have To Become States?", *Philosophers Look at Canadian Confederation*, 23-25.

39.   See Fishman, *Language and Ethnicity in Minority Sociolinguistic Perspective*, 277.

40.   Fishman, *Language and Ethnicity in Minority Sociolinguistic Perspective*, 270.

41.   Tim Connell, "Language and Legislation: The Case of Catalonia", *Journal of Area Studies* 11 (Spring 1985): 12.

42.   On the Galician case, see Catherine Davies, "The Early Formation of a Galician Nationalist Ideology: The Vital Role of the Poet", *Journal of Area Studies* 11 (Spring 1985): 17-21.

43.   Taylor, "Why Do Nations Have To Become States?", 26.

Part II

French Canadians and their Rights

5

The French-Canadian Identity

Language is at the core of French Canada's personality, in and outside Québec. Coalescing with culture, ethnicity, and territory, and for a long time with Roman Catholicism, it embodies the history of a people and its struggle to survive. There is little doubt about that. What is interesting is the story of how this came to be, for it says something about the emergence of the French language as identity itself.

The last chapter addressed the contingency of language as a necessary factor in the preservation of an ethnic and cultural identity. In the late sixties, the federal Commission on Bilingualism and Biculturalism (the so-called Laurendeau-Dunton Commission) concurred, pointing out that in some cases language can be sacrificed without any major loss to ethnic identity. Many Aboriginals, Acadians, and Welsh, it seemed, have "adopted" the English language without abandoning cultural traits and a sense of pride in their ethnic identity.[1] But the Commission also properly noted that the remaining cultural identity, deprived of its link with language, often becomes more vulnerable to further acculturation as generations pass. Furthermore, the view that language is not an essential feature of identity confronts deep-rooted beliefs among French Canadians whose communal membership equates with the French language. Thus the Commission came to the conclusion that cultural identity "is much more than the persistence of a few psychological traits or expressions of folklore" and that the life of the French-Canadian culture necessarily implies the life of the French language.[2]

It is difficult to assess when the French-Canadian identity began to interface primarily with language rather than with other markers of identity, such as ethnicity and religion. One can trace back the existence of a *Canadien* personality (at first the term Canadien referred to French Canadians only) to when the isolation of New France produced a colonial identity distinct from that of the French metropolis. By 1760, the majority of the population of New France was native-born, which means that its inhabitants had a sense of distinctness which at times manifested itself in tensed relations with the French colonial administration and newly arrived settlers born in France. [3] Although it was too early for the French language to be at the root of this growing feeling of distinctness, the Canadien personality was already being shaped by an emerging dialect indigenous to New France that combined the various dialects of the original French settlers. [4]

The British Conquest (1760) in its own way may have served to strengthen the budding Canadien identity. By severing ties with France and opening the colony to immigrants from Great Britain, the Conquest made the Canadiens more acutely aware of their identity and of the urgency to protect it under the new British regime. What is more, the British soon abandoned their policy of assimilation. The initial course of the new British administration had been expressed in the Royal Proclamation of 1763: the French land tenure system was to be abolished, English law imposed, and the Church of England established. Catholics would have to renounce their faith in order to assume office and the Roman Catholic Church would not be allowed to collect tithes. But the need to ensure loyalty from the Canadien elites in the face of threats coming from the south, as well as the openness of Governor James Murray to the French people,[5] convinced the imperial authorities to abandon this policy for a new one. Hence the Quebec Act of 1774 was born. It re-established civil law and the seigneuries, gave the Church the right to collect tithes again, and abolished the oath of allegiance to the Church of England as a prerequisite for assuming office. The new policy was more in tune with the attitude of the British authorities of the time, whose use of the French language not only as a way of communicating with their new subjects, but as a language of work within their own internal administration and correspondence, was apparently not an unusual occurrence. [6] In any case this change of heart amounted to leaving in place the necessary matrix for the growth of the Canadien identity: a society wherein the Church would later emerge as the main institution through which the Catholic faith and the French language could be preserved.

Another event that shaped the French-Canadian identity was the Constitution Act of 1791. The growing Loyalist population who had settled along the Great Lakes demanded a majority status from the Colonial government, not content being a minority in this French-speaking colony. Loyalist immigrants brought along with them sourness and suspicion towards things French and Catholic, and they soon accused French Canadians of plotting against them with Republicans on one hand and papists on the other.[7] This contributed to the erosion of the somewhat amicable relationship between the French and the English that had prevailed until then, thereby occasioning new tensions between the two communities. Moreover, some members of the British Parliament felt that the Canadiens should be allowed to make laws in their own language according to their own customs and particular needs.[8] In response, the 1791 Constitution Act divided the Colony of Québec into Lower and Upper Canada, thus creating an English-Protestant majority in Upper Canada and a French-Catholic majority in Lower Canada, each with its own representative assembly. Although the government of Lower Canada was British-controlled and not accountable to the assembly, the new system nonetheless provided the French-Canadian majority with an assembly in which they would begin to exercise influence, pressure Britain for allowing responsible government, and frustrate the assimilatory attempts of the anglophone minority.[9] In a sense, the Act created a kind of security zone and a territorial enclave for the French-Canadian identity to mature into what was to later become the Québécois political identity.

Following the crushing of the 1837 Rebellions in both Upper and Lower Canada, Lord Durham was sent in from England to investigate unrest in the colony. However true his now famous observation was—"I found two nations warring within the bosom of a single state"—it led him to conclude that assimilating the French-Canadian nation was the solution. In his eyes, French Canadians were "a people with no history and no literature", an "uneducated and unprogressive people". To achieve this goal, the two Canadas would be reunited under a single assembly (Act of Union, 1840) whose main feature was to under-represent French Canada despite its larger population. Consistently with Durham's views, an official policy of assimilation would also be put in place.

Despite these new obstacles, French-Canadian statesmen succeeded in preserving some of the structures of Lower Canada, and the Catholic Church continued to build social and educational institutions. The regime under the Act of Union failed to absorb French Canada, partly because of the modus vivendi which developed soon after 1840 between colonial elites. Still, the inefficient structure of the Union, which led to a political deadlock, and the desire to expand capitalism coast to coast brought together colonial elites who began to devise plans for a new union. Hence modern Canada was born, confederating the former colony of Canada with those of New Brunswick and Nova Scotia. It would give the majority of French Canadians a provincial status with powers over those matters that were considered central to the preservation of their identity, notably the administration of justice, hospitals, education, and the celebration of marriage. As for French-Canadian and Acadian minorities who were to fall under other jurisdictions, their fate was left to the provincial authorities who soon abolished most of their rights and privileges and actively pursued policies of assimilation.

The French-Canadian identity in Québec was bound to the clerical nationalist ideology of *la survivance* (survival) of which faith, traditional values and the French language were the main strands. The defeat of the reformist and secular Patriotes, who had led a rebellion against the British regime in 1837, allowed the Roman Catholic Church to gain considerable influence in French-Canadian society. The Church permeated all social structures (the family, the school, the parish) and performed various institutional functions (education, health care, and social services). That is not to say that French Canada was totally isolated from modern economic life; after all, liberal individualism appears to have been one of the strands of Québec society since late nineteenth century, coexisting with the clerical nationalist ideology of survival.[10] Still, there is little doubt that French Canadians' self-image was, in the words of Lionel Groulx, that of "a little people who have never had much happiness to spare".[11] A little people perhaps, but one which had given itself a grand mission.

It was understood that the French language and Catholicism were intimately tied, and that French Canadians were, in virtue of these ties, the trustees of Christianity in a land where the golden calf was worshipped. God had created different races with different qualities, each with its own contribution to make and, it must be stressed, each with its own language. In *A Sermon on the Vocation of the French Race in America* (1902), Mgr L.-A. Pâquet is eloquently clear on what must be French Canada's contribution:

> Now, my brothers—why should I hesitate to say it—we have the privilege of being entrusted with this social priesthood granted only to select peoples. I cannot doubt that this religious and civilizing mission is the true vocation and the special vocation of the French race in America. Yes, let us not forget, we are not only a civilized race, we are pioneers of a civilization; we are not only a religious people, we are messengers of the spirit of religion; we are not only dutiful sons of the Church, we are, or we should be, numbered among its zealots, its defenders, and its apostles. Our mission is less to handle capital than to stimulate ideas; less to light the furnaces of factories than to maintain and spread the glowing fires of religion and thought, and to help them cast their light into the distance. [12]

The mission can only be accomplished, he argued, if French Canadians are true to themselves, which is to say that their language is a sacred possession that must be protected against those who are "less inspired with the ideal, the kind of feverish mercantilism and vulgar bestiality that rivets them to material things". [13] Henri Bourassa also understood the duty of preserving language as a God-given gift for expressing a people's most noble spirit and character. "When we have lost our language", he wrote in *The French Language and the Future of Our Race* (1912), "we would likely be mediocre Englishmen, passable Scots, or bad Irishmen". [14] Or again, Lionel Groulx warned against the dangers of assimilation which deprives French Canadians of their true nature, hence at the same time deprives Canada of a source of culture and spirituality. [15] Preserving the French language is not so much a matter of right, but a duty to protect the means of spreading Christianity across America. Whether a matter of right or one of duty, at the time the French language could not be understood in isolation from faith. Both were merged into an organic identity.

The clerical ideology dominated Québec until the late 1940's. The radical transformation of Québec society in the post-war period, coined the Quiet Revolution, saw language become the main ingredient of the identity of Québec's French Canadians. The ideological shift from survival to affirmation meant that the Clergy lost its power over education and social services in the face of growing state intervention, namely with the creation of a Ministry of Education. The idea that French Canada's survival, or its moral unity, depends on a "filial obedience to the teachings of the Church and a complete submission to the authority of the leaders who represent among us the power of the Church" [16] lost its appeal. Instead the Québec state became the motor of a new secular order and, unlike the defensive stances that had been taken against the central government's intrusions into provincial jurisdiction, successive Québec governments would from then on make more substantial demands on the Canadian federal system. This "coming of age" represented an erosion of those values that had formed the French-Canadian identity, but left language intact. Significantly, the transformation of Québec society through factors such as industrialization, urbanization, education and openness to the world via radio and television contributed to the growing awareness among francophones of their particular situation in North America, and thus may have contributed to the definition of an identity through differentiation. [17] As Québec society became a modern society not unlike the others, its identity reshaped itself around the French language. The French language, which had been but one of the markers of an overall distinct identity, became the substance of the new identity as the other markers faded away. As Dominique Clift and Sheila Arnopoulos argue, once the belief in a French-Canadian race and rural idealism faded away, language quickly filled the void. [18] Transformations in Québec society eroded much of the Roman Catholic way of life and left language as the source of the French-Canadian identity. The Quiet Revolution having rendered unfashionable references to race and religion, the French language became the central pole of identification, a prime value in and of itself. Although language had always been taken to be one of the main features of the French-Canadian personality, its value increased over time, being no longer merely a vehicle or a marker of a multifarious identity, but being identity *itself*. Thus if language is lost, identity is lost.

The importance we attach to the Quiet Revolution makes us forget that French Canada had always asserted itself, and that the sixties represented no rupture in that regard. To be sure, the extensive use of the state as an instrument of national affirmation was new in Québec. So was the modern economic and technocratic discourse. Here lies the paradox: as French Canadians in Québec learned that the language of money and technology was the key to any successful national affirmation, they lost the traits that had distinguished them from others and that had motivated their struggle to survive. The need to rebuild a modern Québécois identity would become the new challenge.

It is no coincidence if it is during this period of great transformations that the first important pieces of language legislation were enacted. Nationalist discourse reflected one way or another the idea that the promotion of the French language in Québec is indistinguishable from the promotion of the Québécois identity. As René Lévesque wrote in 1968:

> Being ourselves is essentially a matter of keeping and developing a personality that has survived for three and a half centuries. At the core of this personality is the fact that we speak French. Everything else depends on this one essential element and follows from it or leads us infallibly back to it. [19]

The architect of the Charter of the French Language, Camille Laurin, also saw how language and identity were bound:

> This policy [Bill 101] was a priority, since language is the very ground under a people's feet: by it they know themselves and are known; it is rooted in their hearts and allows them to express their identity. [20]

The preamble of Bill 101 itself points out the strength of the language-identity link in Québec: "Whereas the French language, the distinctive language of a people that is in the majority French-speaking, is the instrument by which that people has articulated its identity...".

The French-Canadian identity in Québec, Simon Langlois notes, encompasses more than language to include a sense of we-ness defined by psychological borders and protected by a national government. Language marks and fixes these borders, helping to maintain the integrity of their territorial space—a space which, as we will see in chapter 8, now assumes the status of a distinct political society. This also means that the French Québécois increasingly distinguish themselves from French Canadians living elsewhere in Canada. Outside Québec, the French-Canadian identity evolved differently, having no comparable structures and institutions to face adversity. Though to a lesser degree than in Québec, the Church lost its hold on the daily life of French Canadians. But urbanization and industrialization had a different impact, Langlois explains, since it meant the disruption of homogeneous French communities and increased levels of assimilation. While the French Québécois' sense of identity becomes increasingly territorially based, the French-Canadian identity outside Québec remains primarily founded on ethnicity and language alone. Territorial spacing of language, of course, cannot be possible to the same degree for French Canadians outside Québec, with the exception of the Acadians of New Brunswick. Yet the French-Canadian identity appears to be splitting along provincial lines, as francophones increasingly see themselves as *Fransaskois, Franco-Ontariens*, or *Franco-Manitobains*, rather than seeing themselves as French Canadians. In any case, although both French Québécois and French-Canadian personalities centre on the French language, the two are growing apart as the Québécois identity is rooting itself in a territory with clear psychological borders, thus excluding French Canadians from its sense of we-ness. Whether this exclusion can last is questionable given that the two personalities are ultimately bound through a common language.[21]

The territorial dimension therefore has some impact on identity in virtue of Québec's provincial status. We may still wonder whether territory is in any other way an important factor in shaping identity. A study has indeed suggested that geography is a negligible factor in Québec, and that its importance is sometimes inflated because of the overlap of geographic and ethnic boundaries. It suggests, then, that territorial identification serves a supportive function for the usual cultural labels of identification. For Québec francophones, territory is perceived as being only incidentally related with language.[22]

Territory may play yet another supportive function of ethnolinguistic identity. Fred Donnelly recently brought out how the geography of Québec—at least along the St. Lawrence River, where most Québécois live—is itself different from that of its neighbours.

Without going as far as to claim that the topography of Québec determines the Québécois' sense of distinctness, his point is that it nonetheless physically marks the ethnolinguistic boundaries.[23] Regardless of what an empirical study might reveal about his contention, those who have travelled through the province will instinctively agree.

Besides, the same could be said of modern Acadia located in New Brunswick. A glance at the map shows Acadia in the form of a triangle drawn between Moncton, Edmunston and Caraquet—a triangle whose contours, by the way, would likely constitute the borders of a future Acadian province. In any case, we must remember that Acadians are not French Canadians. True, they have in common the French language, and as minorities face the same challenges that French Canadians face in, say, Ontario. But Acadian culture and history are quite distinct from French-Canadian culture and history.[24]

As early as 1713, Acadians were cut off from France and from New France in virtue of the Treaty of Utrecht which finally ceded Acadia to the British. Refusing to take an oath of allegiance to the British Crown on grounds that they wished to preserve their neutrality, Acadians were deported in 1755. Loaded onto boats—some would be lost at sea—they were shipped off to American colonies and England, and when they could not find asylum, pursued their journey to Louisiana, Québec and the West Indies. Philippe Doucet cites Edmund Burke's reaction to the dispersal:

> We did, in my opinion, most inhumanly and upon pretences, that, in the eye of an honest man, are not worth a farthing, root out this poor, innocent deserving people, whom our utter inability to govern or to reconcile gave us no sort of right to extirpate.[25]

After the Treaty of Paris (1763), many Acadians were allowed to return to the Maritimes on the condition that they would settle in small scattered groups. Finding their land now occupied by the English, they indeed scattered and resettled elsewhere, including in the northeast of what was to become New Brunswick. Until the 1860's, Acadians had little or no collective means to maintain and assert their communal identity. Meanwhile the British authorities pursued their policy of anglicization, most notoriously through anti-Catholic legislation that hindered Acadians' access to schooling, land ownership, and political office. It should come as no surprise, then, if Acadians isolated themselves in a defensive stance. Doucet quotes from a revealing testimony:

> Satisfied that we were allowed to live, without having the little we possessed taken away, we only asked to be ignored and to be allowed to peacefully gather the harvests the good Lord gave to us and our neighbors and to enjoy the light of His sun, which He did not deny us. [26]

The publication of Henry Longfellow's poem *Evangeline* (1847) supplied Acadians with the necessary myths around which collective awareness could grow. It tells the story of Evangeline and Gabriel who are reunited after the Deportation, a story Acadians could relate to. French historian Edme Rameau de Saint Père also contributed to this growing sense of identity by publishing a work on the history of Acadia (1859), noting its distinctness from French-Canadian society. In other words Acadians were being recognized, and through this recognition their sense of identity was reinforced as well as the desire to take control of their own destiny. It also meant increased confrontations against the anglophone-dominated government of New Brunswick, most notably over the issue of education rights.

If Confederation naturally brought closer together the destinies of Canadiens and Acadians, the latter did not for the rest become French Canadians in 1867, nor did they ally themselves to Québec. For one thing, Acadians largely opposed the Confederation scheme which would submerge Acadia in a still larger polity. The project, which seemed to benefit Québec by granting it more autonomy over its own affairs, did not address Acadian concerns. As Doucet notes, in their opposition to Confederation Acadians showed for the first time a united political position, standing apart not only from anglophone New Brunswickers, but from the Québécois as well.

Léon Thériault invokes an event that symbolizes Acadians' wish to remain distinct from Québec, as they had been distinct from New France. After having participated in Québec's *Société Saint-Jean-Baptiste*'s grand meeting of 1880, Acadian leaders decided to hold their own meeting in Memramcook (New Brunswick) one year later. One of the items on the agenda was agreeing on a date for Acadia's national holiday. Proposals to choose the same day as the Québécois' National holiday, Saint-Jean-Baptiste day, were rejected in favour of August 15, the Feast of the Assumption. Other national symbols were soon chosen: the French tricolor enriched with a yellow star in the blue portion became the Acadian flag, and *Ave Maris Stella* became the national anthem. [27]

The Acadian identity consolidated itself in the years that followed these national conventions. The Roman Catholic Church, which had been controlled by anglophones, became increasingly acadianized with the establishment of French parishes and with the nominations of Acadians to the high clergy. The openly nationalist newspaper *L'Évangéline* was founded. Furthermore, the works of genealogists and historians contributed to a better understanding of Acadians' roots.

Any further progress, however, was hindered by the fact that with Confederation Acadia did not fall under a single provincial jurisdiction, but under three: New Brunswick, Nova Scotia, and Prince Edward Island. Most of Lower Canada, as opposed to Acadia, had the advantage of falling only under Québec's jurisdiction. Wherever they were, Acadians seemed condemned to remain a minority at the margins of mainstream anglophone provincial majorities, whereas the French Canadians of Québec would hold a numerical majority. Nonetheless, the industrialization and urbanization that followed the Second World War led to increased government intervention, which would in the sixties begin to include state language planning in New Brunswick, where Acadians constitute an important minority.

There is no doubt that French Canada's identity is not monolithic. Acadians are not French Canadians. They each have their own stories to tell, their own myths and legends to remember. Although this is a truism to most French Canadians and Acadians, it is sometimes overlooked by some anglophones who only see French. Yet their mistake contains a portion of truth that French Canadians and Acadians too often neglect in their attempts to assert their respective identity: they are who they are because they are French. As a matter of fact, their continued existence is bound with the vitality of the French language. Why this justifies strong language rights is what we must now consider.

Notes

1. Report of the Royal Commission on Bilingualism and Biculturalism, *Book I: The Official Languages* (Ottawa: Queen's Printer, 1967), xxxvii.

2. Report of the Royal Commission on Bilingualism and Biculturalism, *Book I: The Official Languages*, xxxviii.

3. Guy Lachapelle et al., *The Quebec Democracy: Structures, Processes and Policies* (Toronto: McGraw-Hill Ryerson, 1993), 4.

4. See Kenneth McRoberts, *Quebec: Social Change and Political Crisis* (Toronto: McClelland and Stewart, 1988), 41.

5. Dominique Clift and Sheila McLeod Arnopoulos, *Le fait anglais au Québec* (Montréal: Libre Expression, 1979), 76.

6. See Clift and Arnopoulos, *Le fait anglais au Québec*, 77.

7. See Clift and Arnopoulos, *Le fait anglais au Québec*, 78.

8. See Clift and Arnopoulos, *Le fait anglais au Québec*, 79.

9. McRoberts, *Quebec: Social Change and Political Crisis*, 49.

10. See Fernande Roy, *Progrès, harmonie, liberté: le libéralisme des milieux d'affaires francophones à Montréal au tournant du siècle* (Montréal: Boréal, 1988).

11. Lionel Groulx, "Why We Are Divided", in *Voices From Quebec* (Toronto: Van Nostrand Reinhold, 1977), 159.

12. Mgr L.-A Pâquet, "A Sermon on the Vocation of the French Race in America", in *French-Canadian Nationalism: An Anthology*, ed. Ramsay Cook (Toronto: Macmillan, 1969), 154.

13. Pâquet, "A Sermon on the Vocation of the French Race in America", 158.

14. Henri Bourassa, "The French Language and the Future of Our Race", in *French-Canadian Nationalism: An Anthology*, 133.

15. Lionel Groulx, "L'Action française", in *Abbé Groulx: Variations on a Nationalist Theme*, ed. Susan Mann Trofimenkoff (Vancouver: Copp Clark Publishing, 1973).

16. Pâquet, "A Sermon on the Vocation of the French Race in America", 159.

17. André Bernard, *La politique au Canada et au Québec* (Sillery: Les Presses de l'Université du Québec, 1982), 94-95.

18. Clift and Arnopoulos, *Le fait anglais au Québec*, 88.

19. René Lévesque, *An Option for Quebec* (Toronto: McClelland and Stewart Limited, 1968), 14.

20. Camille Laurin, "Charte de la langue française", *Revue canadienne de sociologie et d'anthropologie* 15, no. 2 (1978): 121.

21. See Simon Langlois, *La société québécoise en tendances: 1960-1990* (Québec: Institut québécois de recherche sur la culture, 1990), 642-644.

22. See Donald Taylor et al., "Dimensions of Ethnic Identity: An Example From Quebec", *The Journal of Social Psychology* 89 (1973).

23. Fred Donnelly, "Geography Helps Make Quebec Distinct", *Evening Times Globe* (Saint John, NB), Tuesday, 30 August 1994, sec. A, p. 9.

24. Here I follow closely two excellent overviews: Léon Thériault, "Acadia, 1763-1978: An Historical Synthesis", and Philippe Doucet, "Politics and the Acadians", both in *The Acadians of the Maritimes*, ed. Jean Daigle (Moncton: Centre d'études acadiennes, 1982).

25. Edmund Burke, quoted in Doucet, "Politics and the Acadians", 225.

26. Doucet, "Politics and the Acadians", 227.

27. Thériault, "Acadia, 1763-1978: An Historical Synthesis", 70-72.

6

Justifying Strong Language Rights

Whether we are talking about official bilingualism at the federal level, Québec's Bill 101, or New Brunswick's Bill 88, community rights such as these are often perceived as illiberal attacks on universal moral rights that protect autonomy.[1] While it is true that an important strand of democratic tradition is conceived along those lines, it tends to obfuscate the justifications for these rights. Anglophones living in North America do not need to think about protecting the English language simply because market forces always privilege the dominant linguistic group. Moreover, allophone immigrants will choose to learn English as the dominant language in order to maximize their chances of integration and upward mobility. This process guarantees a continued supply (so to speak) of new anglophones and brings further pressures to assimilate all linguistic minorities, including French. Given these demolinguistic conditions, how could the Québec state afford to be culturally neutral? How could the New Brunswick government not recognize community rights for Acadia? The rationale for state intervention in linguistic matters is no different from the rationale for intervening in matters such as social welfare, education, the environment and security: market forces benefit the powerful and, in this particular case, are incapable of sustaining linguistic minorities and of fostering proper relations between the various language groups of a given polity.[2]

Many will object to such arguments, invoking the danger that strong language rights pose to individual freedoms. Language rights, they will say, should be limited to the protection of some of the conditions for personal autonomy, such as the right to freedom of action within one's own private affairs. These would include the rights against undue interference in private language use and against discrimination on the basis of language. Few are those who will deny us the right to speak our language at home and on the streets, to use it in letters and on the telephone, to keep our native names and surnames, to use our language within our cultural and religious institutions, newspapers, radio stations, and community centres. We could also add to this list the right to an interpreter in judicial proceedings, a language right derived from the right to a fair trial.

Why are these language rights more easily defensible? Because they are typically associated with state tolerance, or, put differently, they are rights *against* state interference rather than ones that require a positive state intervention. The right not to be interfered with within one's private sphere of language activity and that of not being discriminated against on the basis of language are derived from the right to privacy and fairness, respectively. They can be grounded in the interests of all citizens of a liberal polity, regardless of their particular community status. Were I the last person speaking my language, I would still have the right against undue interference and discrimination. For our purposes such rights can be called negative language rights, for the duties they involve are negative duties: *not* interfering in a person's language use, and treating everyone equally *regardless* of the language spoken.

Negative language rights are recognized in the International covenant on civil and political rights.[3] Section 26 reads as follows:

> All persons are equal before the law and are entitled without any discrimination to equal protection of the law. In this respect the law shall prohibit any discrimination and guarantee to all persons equal and effective protection against discrimination on any ground such as race, color, sex, *language*, religion, political or other opinion, national or social origin, birth or other status. [my emphasis]

Moreover, section 27 states:

> In those States in which ethnic, religious or linguistic minorities exist, persons belonging to such minorities shall not be denied the right, *in community with the other members of their group*, to enjoy their own culture, to profess and practise their own religion, or to use their own language. [my emphasis]

There is no explicit recognition of the right against discrimination on the basis of language in the Canadian Charter of Rights and Freedoms. Section 15 of the Charter includes protection against discrimination on the basis of race, national or ethnic origin, color, religion, sex, age or mental or physical disability, but *not* on the basis of language. However, section 10 of the Québec Charter of Human Rights and Freedoms (Québec's own provincial charter of rights, in place since 1974), unlike its Canadian counterpart, does include language in its list of items that ought to be protected against discrimination.

Nor is there any explicit protection against state interference in private language use. Presumably, using one's language in one's private sphere could indirectly be protected in the Charter via freedom of association. Being free to associate with whomever I want entails that I can join with others who speak my language, whether it be casually on the sidewalk or formally in a community centre. The state having no business in preventing us from associating, it has no more business in preventing us from speaking our language.

The recognition of language rights is partly derived from section 2 of the Charter which guarantees fundamental freedoms such as freedom of expression. In *A. G. Quebec v La chaussure Brown's* [1988], the Supreme Court of Canada interpreted the freedom of expression guarantees of section 2(b) of the Charter to include the freedom to express oneself in the language of one's choice:

> Language is so intimately related to the form and content of expression that there cannot be true freedom of expression by means of language if one is prohibited from using the language of one's choice. Language is not merely a means or medium of expression; it colors the content and meaning of expression. [4]

As we shall see in the next chapter, the Human Rights Committee of the United Nations also put forth this linkage between speaking one's language and expressing oneself, invoking section 19(2) of the International covenant on civil and political rights, which reads as follows:

Everyone shall have the right to freedom of expression; this right shall include
freedom to seek, receive and impart information and ideas of all kinds,
regardless of frontiers, either orally, in writing or in print, in the form of art,
or through any other media of his choice.

Advocates of linguistic laissez-faire insist that these language rights
are quite sufficient, and that surely no one could reasonably assert
additional language rights in virtue of being members of a particular
community. At best, this kind of discourse is consistent with liberal
tradition and its emphasis on personal autonomy and equality of
citizens. At worse, it conceals hegemonic projects.

Positive state intervention is necessary to promote minority
languages, for their vulnerability in a free market environment cannot
be disputed. Unrestrained competition between languages will not
bring about linguistic harmony, but a subordination of minority
languages to the dominant language, and a subordination of the
minority community to the dominant community. The idea of state
neutrality is deceitful in this context, for laissez-faire de facto prejudices
the dominant language in terms of its use and status. According to
Catherine Philipponneau, a policy of non-intervention is often nothing
more than an undeclared policy of assimilation.[5] Joshua Fishman
describes the supposedly "free" market as the unrestrained clash of
unequal forces governed by the law of the jungle. Those in a dominant
position have a vested interest in defending the myth that the market
reflects a universal and inevitable principle and that organizing against
it to stay alive amounts to interfering with the laws of nature.[6] The
view that only negative language rights could be justified is rooted in a
universalism that conceives of positive state interventions as violations
of rights that protect individual autonomy. The free market indeed
assumes an air of sanctity when its laws are concealed in the guise of
some imprescriptible universal moral law, one that gives birth to
individual rights. Camille Laurin, the architect of Québec's Bill 101,
felt that invoking universalism to justify laissez-faire and formal
individual rights only serves the interests of the dominant group,
especially when the concrete inequalities between languages and peoples
are not taken into account.[7] Clearly the discourse on laissez-faire is not
convincing, and minorities who wish to protect their languages have

little to rejoice if their only acceptable recourse is an appeal to the right against interference and discrimination.

There are also those who believe that community members alone should bear the responsibility of promoting their own language, and that the state and outsiders are not morally bound to assist. Language planning is permissible, they say, but only to the extent that its costs be born by community members themselves. Non-members should not be the unconsenting victims of language planning, and public resources certainly should not be used to that effect. And, after all, is it not true that if a linguistic community is on the decline, community members should blame their own inaction and behaviour, not the free market of languages? On the surface this argument may sound convincing, but appealing to the individual's responsibility for preserving his own language is a chimera. [8] To claim that individual responsibility is enough to maintain the more fragile language communities is to ignore how subtle and pernicious the process of assimilation can be. Members of a minority language community too often "choose" the dominant group's language for reasons that have nothing to do with a genuine wish to integrate in mainstream society or to ensure upward mobility. It is much more the community's lack of expressive power and recognition and, mostly, it is a lack of self-respect which provokes these unauthentic and alienated "choices". [9]

There is another reason why non-interference does little to promote linguistic minorities. Language is significantly different from other markers of identity, say ethnicity or religion, against which discrimination often occurs. As Kenneth McRae writes, "[s]ocieties characterized by linguistic pluralism differ from those characterized by racial, religious, class or ideological divisions in one essential respect, which stems from the pervasive nature of language as a general vehicle of communication". [10] State neutrality just does not have the same effect on language. Language practice being necessarily communicative, unlike racial origin or religious beliefs, it always requires social interaction and thus involves greater demands on others. [11]

The point I am raising is not that the rights against undue interference and discrimination on the basis of language are harmful or useless. Rather, it is to say that such rights are more easily defensible in liberal society, being derived from our interests in privacy and fairness, two goods which are ultimately derived from the value of personal autonomy. The negative duties these narrowly defined rights involve are also the only ones that can be imposed on the state with the expectation that they will be fulfilled towards everyone equally. The problem, as has been illustrated, is that such weak language rights are insufficient to sustain more vulnerable languages. Could stronger special language rights, including a whole range of positive action, from various government services to the right to live in one's language, find justification in French Canada?

As far as Québec is concerned, the reasons for active state language planning are many, but most are primarily socioeconomic: despite its solid majority status—approximately 80% of the Québécois have had French as a mother tongue during this century—French was long subordinate to English, especially in the economy where English was the language of those who held economic power. Before state intervention, French was used in the lower echelons of economic life, while English was used in the upper echelons, and so bilingualism was experienced differently depending if one was French- or English-speaking: "The social pressures for using French as a language of communication at work are more strongly felt by lower status anglophones, while the pressures to use English increases as francophones rise in the corporate world".[12] In this cultural division of labour, the subordinate position of the French language and the subordinate position of French Canadians appeared as two sides of the same coin since francophones and anglophones were not equals in the economic realm. In short, French would tend to be relegated to the private sphere, in the homes, schools, and churches. Its inferior status in other spheres was apparent, as Alexis de Tocqueville noted about the language of commercial signs during his visit in 1831: "Dans cette portion du Canada, on n'entend point l'anglais. La population n'est que française, et cependant lorsqu'on rencontre une auberge, ou un marchand, son enseigne est en anglais". [In this portion of Canada, we do not hear any English. The population is French only, and yet when we come across a hotel, or a shop, its sign is in English].[13]

This situation was compounded by the widely held belief that even in French-speaking Québec English is the language of prestige. As Gérard Bergeron notes, it was natural to believe so when generations after generations saw that all important things happen in English, and that knowing English opens the doors to the good life.[14] Moreover, a study comparing French- and English-speakers of equal education and job status revealed that English-speakers were perceived by both anglophones *and* francophones as being more intelligent, having a better job and a higher education.[15] The inferiority complex of French Canadians, reflecting a low self-esteem, led some to despise their origins and to identify with the Anglo-American lifestyle. There was some truth to the idea that capital spoke English and labour spoke French, and linguistic identity and self-esteem were certain to suffer from it. Not surprisingly, diagnosing this disequilibrium motivated a corresponding state intervention.

Another reason for state language planning remains the need to respond to demolinguistic factors which threaten Québec's relative weight in the federation, not to mention French Canada's cultural security within Québec itself. The decline of Québec's population relatively to the Canadian whole translates itself into a greater minority status for Québec within the federation. Québec's share of members of Parliament went from 33,5% in 1867 to 25,4% in 1990, and is expected to go down to 20% or less in about a century.[16] In addition to weakening Québec's political power in the federation, the demographic decline of the Québécois population of French origins creates a cultural insecurity insofar as traditional cultural traits are lost.

Jacques Henripin cites three demographic challenges facing Québec. First, the birth rate of the Québécois (1,6 children per couple) is inferior to the required rate for replacing generations (2 children per couple); as a result, the population is growing old. A second problem is the high emigration rate towards other provinces. Anglophones leave Québec at a rate fifteen times higher than francophones, allophones (those who have neither French nor English as a mother tongue) at a rate five times higher. This means that immigration, despite what is often believed, contributes little to counteracting the low birth rate since Québec must accept three immigrants in order to keep one. A third problem relates to the difficult integration of immigrants in Montreal, in part because of the attraction that the English language has there. English is still the language which most immigrants adopt, although the situation is improving.[17]

Before Bill 101, immigrant parents, especially those living in Montreal, would often choose English as the language of schooling for their children. In 1970, 8.3% of students in Montreal's English schools were French, while only 1.9% of students in French schools were English. Significantly, 22.5% of students in English schools were allophones, compared to merely 0.9% in French schools.[18] And in 1961, language transfers of allophones toward French were in the proportion of 23.2% in Montreal, as compared with 56.6% in the rest of Québec.[19] Between 1945 and 1966, 80% of immigrants integrated into the anglophone community of Québec, the great majority of them in Montreal.[20]

Various studies and governmental reports have concurred that these concerns were and still are legitimate, and thus that there are grounds for taking steps to ensure that the French language is protected in Québec, namely by sending a unequivocal message to immigrants: French, not English, is the majority language in Québec. Even the Supreme Court of Canada argued that the circumstances discussed above "favored the use of the English language despite the predominance in Quebec of a francophone population ... prior to the enactment of the legislation at issue [Bill 101]...".[21] No one seriously challenges the difficulties French is facing in Québec; what is debated is the scope of language legislation and its impact on other language rights.

As can be expected, Acadians also have had to face major sociodemographic obstacles, but with little or no collective means at their disposal. Assimilation has reached high levels in Prince Edward Island and Nova Scotia, where by 1961 the majority of those of French extraction no longer declared French as their mother tongue. And of those who could still speak French, less than 40% spoke it at home by 1971![22]

Muriel Roy discusses the precarious linguistic conditions in Acadia. The high birth rate, which had compensated for the losses due to out-migration, began to fall in the 1960's. The relative weight of Acadians in the population as a whole therefore cannot be maintained. Furthermore, since the 1940's there are less and less people of French origins who speak French, either because they never had French as a mother tongue, or because they eventually lost the ability to speak it. It is also clear that there is a correlation between density and assimilation rates. For example in New Brunswick—where the overall assimilation rate of Acadians is lowest at 8%—the anglicization rate in the French counties is as low as 1,4%, compared to as high as 51,5% in the English counties. Furthermore, there is also a correlation between increasing urbanization and higher rates of assimilation. Finally, one of the most damaging factors that plays against the retention of French is exogamous marriages. The francophone, in all probability, must accommodate his or her anglophone unilingual spouse by switching to English at home, which also means that their children are unlikely to learn French. [23] Be that as it may, most agree that the Acadians of New Brunswick are in a far more envious position than French Canadians outside Québec, where the rate of assimilation tends to increase as the distance from Québec increases. As Ronald Wardhaugh writes, "[n]o objective assessment of the situation of the French outside Quebec can escape the conclusion that almost everywhere they face the danger of linguistic and cultural extinction". [24]

Conditions such as those that prevail in French Canada show how reliance on non-interference and non-discrimination is insufficient, and justify more extensive language planning. With respect to Québec, state language planning serves two major functions: to improve the quality and correctness of Québec French (corpus planning) and to improve its socioeconomic position in Québec society (status planning). For example, since the early sixties Québec has had a French language bureau whose function is (among other things) to find French versions of English loan words brought by new technology. More closely related to status planning are the various laws (such as Bill 22 and Bill 101) which aimed at giving the French language a majority status within Québec. If corpus and status planning are considered different types of interventions, it must be remembered that promoting the status of a language goes hand in hand with promoting its quality, as has certainly been the case in Québec. Simply put, why bother with measures that advance the status of a language if little is done to improve its quality in everyday use? It is deplorable, in that regard, that New Brunswick's interventions have neglected the importance of corpus planning, thus leaving Acadians insecure about the worth of the French they speak despite the gains made at the level of status planning, namely with the constitutional entrenchment of their language rights. Acadians have an urgent need for a *Conseil de la langue acadienne* that would oversee not only status planning in New Brunswick, but corpus planning as well. [25] Elsewhere in Canada where the French language is withering away, attempts at reviving French are modest, but still involve active state intervention through policies such as official bilingualism at the federal level, and in rare cases basic services for Francophones at the provincial level.

Canada is of course not the only country involved in language planning. The *Académie française* (French Academy of France) is also responsible for creating new terminology in the context of a rapidly changing technology. In other countries language revival is sometimes achieved by restoring an ancestral language to its former status, for example by reintroducing it into the educational system and the media. At a point where the Hebrew language was no longer anyone's mother tongue, Israel intervened successfully so that it became the main language for a majority of the population. With somewhat less success, many other languages are being revived in the context of movements of national affirmation: Welsh, Irish, and Scottish in the U. K.; Breton, Corsican, and Flemish in France; Catalan and Basque in Spain; Frisian in Holland. [26]

We could add to this list the language law that French culture minister Jacques Toubon introduced in the National Assembly in 1994. The intent of the law was to ban a number of English loan words that, as we all know, are too readily used by the French who have a singular admiration for American English. Interestingly, the Constitutional Council of France ordered the French government to water down the law, citing freedom of expression guarantees found in the 1789 Declaration of the Rights of Man. The government has no right, the Council ruled, to tell private citizens what words they can utter.

In any case, we are talking about active state support of certain linguistic communities, rather than a simple laissez-faire approach that abandons languages to an unfair competition. Where rights are involved, we are talking, then, of a community right, one which is claimed by members of a given community on the grounds that the protection of their language is central to their communal membership and identity. If liberal ideology is comfortable with the weaker negative language rights, those that are held by everyone in virtue of being citizens of the liberal polity, it becomes suspicious of those rights that are claimed by people in virtue of a concurrent membership. The promotion of a community's language through a far-reaching state intervention escapes traditional individual rights-discourse, but can find a place in an improved definition of what community rights are about.

These stronger language rights vary widely in scope. At a minimum, they include the educational rights and services for French- and English-speaking minorities as defined in the Official Languages Act and as guaranteed in the Charter. They also include a variety of services dispensed by provinces to their respective minorities, such as Ontario's Bill 8 which provides francophones with services in their language where numbers warrant, and Québec's legislation which guarantees access to medical and social services in English. It may be objected that these provincial services are not rights, but privileges based on political considerations. However, for our purposes they should be included in the list of services that count as rights, regardless of their lack of constitutional recognition as such. The important point is that these services are ultimately founded on a recognition that the two official language communities are owed a certain protection, which is to say that they are essentially rights, even though they receive little or no constitutional protection.

Other more far-reaching language rights require that one's language be used and understood in a variety of everyday situations, both private and public. They involve considerable financial and human resources beyond the directing of limited public funds to specific institutions. Québec's language policies that give expressive powers to members of the French-speaking majority so that French can remain the language of everyday life reflect such rights. Because of what they are meant to achieve, they must reach further than other language rights. Yet it is important to remember that despite these differences in scope, a characteristic is common to all such state interventions: they are the expression of community rights, rights which individuals have as members of one of the official minority language communities or of the French-Canadian community of Québec.

The problem, it will be noted, is that the exercise of some of these stronger language rights is mutually exclusive. Securing to community

X the conditions for living in its language would presumably raise the issue of securing the same to community *Y*, and to community *Z*, and so on. Fulfilling such duties is impossible because reciprocity is impracticable. Michael MacMillan writes that

> [w]hen a government seeks to acknowledge a strong claim to A's language rights, it necessarily involves a denial of B's claim. By legislating that all public speech must be in language A, it prevents language B from attaining the status of a *lived* language. [27]

Some will conclude that such strong claims could not possibly be justified, for not all individuals can live in their own language. Surely the immigrant who claims the right to speak and be understood in his own minority language will face this opinion. His claim is unfeasible because the universal reciprocity of rights and duties it implies would render the different claims mutually exclusive. The only way that the state can uphold its duty to all linguistic groups equally, whatever their number, is through weak language rights. The duties these rights call for are negative, the kind that can be fulfilled towards everyone equally. To be understood in one's language, it is said, goes beyond moral duties of justice, beyond the right against undue interference and discrimination on the basis of language.

It is true that only the negative right against discrimination and interference on the basis of language can be held by all individuals, for its justification rests on membership in the liberal polity. That should not mean, however, that stronger claims made by particular communities have no valid basis. Notably for historical reasons, some communities hold a special place in a given polity. Indigenous communities obviously come to mind. Even the right to live in one's language can be feasible for territorially based communities which have a certain critical mass in addition to historical claims.

Territory indeed appears as a deciding factor in the implementation of language policy. It is reasonable to assume, with Jean Laponce, that the right to live in one's language is not a transportable right and will therefore most likely be territorially based. The rationale behind territorial language rights is to create a security zone in which a community can determine its linguistic environment within its own borders. As Laponce puts it, the territorial approach allows goods, capital, and persons to freely move within a country, but not language: it remains confined in a strictly delineated zone whose rigid boundaries provide a sense of security to the minority.[28] The territorial approach has gained popularity in the last decades, as witnessed by the numerous references to the Swiss model. There, for instance, educational language rights are territorial: the language of instruction is exclusively that of the Canton (unless it decides otherwise), even if it includes important linguistic minorities. And in the four Cantons which make exception to this rule by allowing additional languages of instruction, these are limited to special unilingual linguistic zones within each Canton. The territorial principle also applies in Belgium, divided into a Dutch-speaking area and a French-speaking area, each having control over its own language policy. Brussels is the exception, being a bilingual zone made up of a majority of francophones, but located in the Dutch-speaking half of Belgium.

Bill 101 is such an extensive right that it would of course be hard to defend were francophones a small and dispersed minority on the Québec territory. It is the presence of a critical mass on a given territory which makes these strong language rights practicable. However, Québec's case does not reflect a pure territorial model, since language and educational rights for the anglophone minority are upheld by both central and provincial governments, not to mention constitutional guarantees. On the one hand, the English-speaking Québécois carries with him official language rights as well as the various provincial rights conferred on him as a member of the anglophone minority. The Charter of Rights and Freedoms guarantees him certain minority language educational rights and rights to receive services in English from federal institutions. The Québec government itself, since Bill 142 (1986), gives anglophones the right to receive social and health services in English where the numbers warrant. On the other hand, the French-speaking Québécois is guaranteed the right to communicate in French within various spheres of life, a right that is rooted in the geographic space considered to be the home of the French language. Even though French Canadians are a minority in Canada and on the continent, it is understood that within the Québec borders they form the majority and *should have the status of a majority*. The territorial approach therefore allows the French-speaking community to hold strong language rights and ensures that immigrants integrate into the linguistic majority, while the personal approach bestows special language rights on the members of the anglophone and Aboriginal communities.

New Brunswick's language policy also appears to be evolving towards a combination of both territorial and personal models of language rights. All citizens of New Brunswick can receive provincial services in either official language. But the territorial principle comes in with the implementation of duality, where people could for example work in their own language within their own milieu. It is felt that only through the creation of autonomous linguistic spheres where the French language predominates can Acadians really hope to live in French. [29]

French Canada's low demographic weight in other parts of Canada, plus the inadequate institutional development and government support in many provinces, largely explains its disintegration. Of course language rights that would attempt to reverse this trend cannot be as extensive as those found in Québec and Acadia, where the right to live in French is defensible. Yet recourse to far-reaching language rights is justifiable for historical reasons, although they generally are not purely modeled on the territorial principle. Language rights for French-speaking Canadians outside Québec are generally based on a mix of the territorial and personal principles in the sense that all individuals have transportable rights to certain services in French, but only where the numbers warrant. For example, section 20(1) of the Canadian Charter of Rights guarantees French language services with federal institutions where there is significant demand. Moreover, section 23(3) states that the right to French language instruction applies wherever there is a sufficient number of eligible children. Thus, even though the right is held by individual French Canadians wherever they are, "significant demand" and "sufficient number" implies a certain territorial concentration before the right may be exercised in effect. [30]

Combining personal and territorial principles sometimes produces complex results. This is inevitable if stronger language rights are to be exercised. It will be noticed, too, that these are all communal language rights, even if they do not have the same reach: they are all rights held by people as members of particular communities. The hard question is, why some communities and not others?

Far-reaching language rights in French Canada largely arise out of an historical transaction between communities. The language rights of French Canadians, Henri Bourassa used to say early this century, are rooted in obligations that arise from the past. French Canadians defended the British Crown and its institutions against American invasions on more than one occasion and continue to act as a buffer against American influence today. In return for their loyalty, services and sacrifices, they are owed the right to flourish across Canada and under the institutions they fought to preserve, which implies the right to an equal status. [31] But even if we leave out Bourassa's views, we can still say that the French language should be equal to English in the public sphere, as one of the two public languages of the Canadian polity. It should be plain to all that the French and the Aboriginal peoples did not immigrate into a predominantly English political community, and therefore unlike other linguistic groups have a stronger claim to protect their language. There is a tacit agreement between a political community and its immigrants that they will learn the majority language and will have no a priori communal claims to strong language rights. French Canadians and Acadians not being immigrants in the same sense, they can make historical claims to refuse linguistic integration and to receive protection from the state. That the legitimacy of community language rights in Canada is rooted in history makes no doubt.

It might still be asked, "But what of other communities which have also made their contribution? Are they not owed the same rights?". Since the above arguments revolve around the claim that French Canadians and Acadians have special rights in virtue of some historical priority, it is understanding that they sometimes fail to persuade other ethnic minorities who feel that their own language is treated as a second-class language, hence that they themselves are treated as second-class citizens. I do not deny that it is desirable to sustain a degree of plurality of languages and to be sensitive to the linguistic composition of regions. Official multiculturalism attempts to provide for this. And as was suggested by the Laurendeau-Dunton Commission, not only is it entirely reasonable that other languages should be included in the school curriculum and used in private institutions, in some cases they should also receive local legal recognition.[32] Still, not all communities can claim the same language rights equally, since there are moral grounds for allocating public funds to the active promotion of some communities more than others. In its list of recommendations to include the use of languages other than French or English in schools, universities, the media, and the arts, the Laurendeau-Dunton Commission does not speak of a duty of justice towards these "non-official" minorities, but rather of a duty of benevolence.[33] In other words, ethnic minorities other than French and English are not owed stronger language rights. Only the negative rights against undue interference and discrimination on the basis of language apply to all as a matter of justice. No doubt some will object to such a position towards ethnic groups other than French and English, yet it may be the only defensible, let alone practicable, one in the Canadian context.

That official bilingualism is an unjustifiable use of public funds which favours only the French to the detriment of all those other ethnic groups is not only an unreasonable view, but may also play against these ethnic groups. On the surface it has moral force because it speaks of equal treatment and denounces privileges, and thus will find sympathetic ears amongst members of other ethnic minorities. But it often conceals a rejection of official multiculturalism, too. Those who object to bilingualism often do so because they fear differences and are unable to reconcile themselves with the loss of their hegemony over society. Needless to say it is an attitude that is not receptive to multiculturalism and the maintaining of differences. There is no way that the cultural imperialists who wrap themselves in the language of moral outrage in denouncing bilingualism will open their arms to multiculturalism. Assuming both to be sectarian demands injurious to liberal society and Canadian uniformity, they will in lieu propose putting an end to any such official recognition and use of public funds. They will, in other words, profess their tolerance towards a diversity of cultures and languages, so long as such diversity is consigned to the private sphere. Ethnic minorities ought to be cautious when they too oppose official bilingualism, for they may be unwillingly supporting the attitude that will turn against them.

The idea of compensatory justice also comes into play. Being the victim of past—and ongoing—injustice perhaps is not an independent justification for holding rights. But it does raise the urgency of the claims. For Camille Laurin, who sees the Charter of the French Language as a statement of fundamental rights, language legislation was a priority not only because of the presence of a strong language-identity link, but also

> because the quality of our language is threatened by the decay resulting from the colonization of the people of Québec, and because their rights must be restored to those who have suffered discrimination and injustice simply for speaking the language of their country. [34]

This applies even more to French Canadians and Acadians who live outside Québec. Confederation was meant to re-associate both communities into a new polity, one that would effectively end Durham's policy of assimilation that was in place under the Act of Union. The oppression of French Canadians and Acadians that followed soon after 1867 in all provinces largely contributed to their erosion as a community. Since the original pact had been broken, of which tacit language rights were an integral part, denying claims to compensatory justice constitutes a further affront to the terms of Confederation.

There is much to be said for the validity of mutual obligations that arise out of past experiences, and the seriousness of the injury that is committed when one community is blind to its duties. Canadians' language rights are, in that sense, not only an expression of how they ought to be treated as citizens of the liberal polity, bearers of individual language rights against undue interference and discrimination on the basis of language, but can also be the expression of how they ought to be treated as members of a linguistic community, bearers of stronger community rights. The widely recognized liberal principle that we should respect individual language rights is complemented by the notion that the domain of communal identity constitutes a substantive value equally worthy of respect. We can look upon this as moral progress, as I see it, or we can denounce what on the surface appears like a potential loss of personal autonomy. If I am correct, our views on language conflicts in Canada must be reassessed in order to account for the proper moral weight of each claim and the nature of the tensions that inevitably arise from their coexistence.

Notes

1. Parts of this chapter elaborate on my previously published article "Language Rights, Individual and Communal", *Language Problems and Language Planning* 17, no. 2 (Summer 1993).

2. See Richard Bourhis, "Introduction: Language Policies in Multilingual Settings", *Conflict and Language Planning in Quebec*, ed. Richard Y. Bourhis (Philadelphia: Multilingual Matters, 1984), 2.

3. The International covenant on civil and political rights can be found in *World Human Rights Guide*, ed. Charles Humana (Oxford: Oxford University Press, 1992).

4. Supreme Court of Canada, *The Attorney General of Quebec v La Chaussure Brown's Inc.*, 37.

5. Catherine Philipponneau, "Politique et aménagement linguistiques au Nouveau-Brunswick: Pour de nouvelles stratégies d'intervention", in *Vers un aménagement linguistique de l'Acadie du Nouveau-Brunswick*, ed. Catherine Philipponneau (Moncton: Centre de recherche en linguistique appliquée, 1991), 52.

6. Joshua Fishman, "Conference Comments: Reflections on the Current State of Language Planning", *Actes du Colloque international sur l'aménagement linguistique*, 412.

7. Laurin, "Charte de la langue française", 124-125.

8. For example, see Jean-Claude Corbeil, "Commentaire de la communication de Sélim Abou: 'Éléments pour une théorie générale de l'aménagement linguistique'", *Actes du Colloque international sur l'aménagement linguistique*, 20. He writes the following:

"[N]ous avons constaté que l'individu, laissé à lui-même, est incapable d'influencer l'évolution d'une situation de multilinguisme, qu'au contraire, il subit la dynamique des forces en présence; lui tenir le discours de sa prétendue responsabilité ne peut que développer chez lui le sentiment de son impuissance, d'où une frustration qui peut devenir explosive sur le plan politique, ou l'abandon pur et simple de son identité linguistique."

9. See Taylor, "Why do Nations Have to Become States?"

10. Kenneth D. McRae, "Bilingual Language Districts in Finland and Canada: Adventures in the Transplanting of an Institution", *Canadian Public Policy* 4, no. 3 (Summer 1978): 331.

11. See Laponce, *Langue et territoire*, 147, where he writes:

"Il est facile et raisonnable de dire 'vous serez admis ou promu quelle que soit votre race ou votre religion' sans pour cela rien changer aux institutions existantes; mais comment pourrait-on dire la même chose, dans les mêmes conditions de statu quo, lorsqu'il s'agit de la langue parlée? Une langue ... ne saurait se penser autrement qu'en terme de locuteurs capables de se comprendre. Zolberg le dit fort bien: l'État peut jouer l'aveugle, non pas le sourd-muet."

12. Pierre Laporte, "Status Language Planning in Quebec: An Evaluation", in *Conflict and Language Planning in Quebec*, ed. Richard Y. Bourhis (Philadelphia: Multilingual Matters, 1984), 57.

13. Alexis de Toqueville, quoted by Gérard Bergeron, *Pratique de l'État au Québec* (Montréal: Québec/Amérique, 1984), 120. My translation.

14. Bergeron, *Pratique de l'État au Québec*, 120.

15. See Denise Daoust-Blais, "Corpus and Status Language Planning in Quebec: A Look at Linguistic Education", in *Progress in Language Planning*, ed. Juan Cobarrubias and Joshua Fishman (Berlin: Walter de Gruyter, 1983), 210.

16. Rodrigue Tremblay, "Le statut politique et constitutionnel du Québec" in *Commission sur l'avenir politique et constitutionnel du Québec*, Document de travail numéro 4 (Québec: Bibliothèque nationale du Québec, 1991), 1014.

17. Jacques Henripin, "Réponses aux questions posées par la Commission sur l'avenir politique et constitutionnel du Québec" in *Commission sur l'avenir politique et constitutionnel du Québec*, Document de travail numéro 4 (Québec: Bibliothèque nationale du Québec, 1991), 454.

18. Laporte, "Status Language Planning in Quebec: An Evaluation", 57.

19.   Daoust-Blais, "Corpus and Status Language Planning in Quebec: A Look at Linguistic Education", 209.

20.   Bergeron, *Pratique de l'État au Québec*, 122.

21.   Supreme Court of Canada, *The Attorney General of Quebec v La Chaussure Brown's Inc.*, 72.

22.   Thériault, "Acadia, 1763-1978: An Historical Synthesis", 84.

23.   Muriel K. Roy, "Settlement and Population Growth in Acadia", in *The Acadians of the Maritimes*, 177-183.

24.   Ronald Wardhaugh, *Language and Nationhood: The Canadian Experience* (Vancouver: New Star Books, 1983), 108.

25.   Philipponneau, "Politique et aménagement linguistiques au Nouveau-Brunswick: Pour de nouvelles stratégies d'intervention", 59. Also see Gérard Snow's comment in "Quelles structures d'aménagement linguistique pour l'Acadie du Nouveau-Brunswick: bilinguisme, dualité, régionalisation?", in *Vers un aménagement linguistique de l'Acadie du Nouveau-Brunswick*, 171-172.

26.   Bourhis, "Introduction: Language Policies in Multilingual Settings", 4-10.

27.   Michael MacMillan, "Language Rights, Human Rights and Bill 101, *Queen's Quarterly* 90 (Summer 1983): 351.

28.   Laponce, *Langue et territoire*, 141-142.

29.   See Jean-Denis Gendron, "L'autonomie linguistique dans le cadre de l'aménagement linguistique du Nouveau-Brunswick", in *Vers un aménagement linguistique de l'Acadie du Nouveau-Brunswick*, 155-156.

30.   Many have observed that linguistic concentration appears inevitable: Québec is becoming more French, while the rest of Canada is becoming more English. Language policy, some conclude, must adapt itself to this reality, for example by favouring the territorial model. Others add that this model also has the advantage of being cheaper. On the latter, see Neil B. Ridler and Suzanne Pons-Ridler, "An Economic Analysis of Canadian Language Policies: A Model and Its Implementation", *Language Problems and Language Planning* 10 (1986), and "The Territorial Concept of Official Bilingualism; A Cheaper Alternative for Canada?", *Language Sciences* 11 (1989).

31.   Bourassa, "The French Language and the Future of Our Race", 134-136. On Henri Bourassa's views on language rights, see Michael MacMillan, "Henri Bourassa on the Defence of Language Rights", *Dalhousie Review* 62 (Fall 1982).

32.   Report of the Royal Commission on Bilingualism and Biculturalism, *Book IV: The Cultural Contribution of the Other Ethnic Groups* (Ottawa: Queen's Printer, 1969), 13.

33.   Report of the Royal Commission on Bilingualism and Biculturalism, *Book IV: The Cultural Contribution of the Other Ethnic Groups*, 228-230.

34.   Laurin, "Charte de la langue française", 121.

7

Québec and Bill 101

In the previous chapter we examined some of the socioeconomic and demolinguistic conditions that contribute to the erosion of the French language in Canada.[1] They motivate various degrees of state language planning whose ultimate aims are cultural as well as political: to sustain the conditions for a communal identity based on the French language and to preserve Québec's weight within the federation—assuming that these two ultimately reinforce each other. In that respect, Québec's Charter of the French language (Bill 101) has gone further than any other piece of language legislation, sparking endless bickering about its legitimacy. How can a law that simply helps a people work and play in its own majority language be so controversial?

Language planning in Québec did not begin with Bill 101. Already in 1910, a law forced public utility companies to include a French version of their printed material alongside the English version. Later in 1937, the government of Maurice Duplessis passed legislation that gave priority to the French version of laws, a controversial measure that was withdrawn one year later. If these laws were rather timid and benign, there existed nonetheless a real concern about the status of the French language, a concern strongly expressed by nationalists like Lionel Groulx who in 1918 wrote the following:

> How could strangers travelling in our province or in our cities not believe in our abdication and our disappearance when so many French Canadians hide their French origins behind English signs, when railroad companies spread the network of their English geography over the French countryside? What tourist, for example, could have guessed the existence of a French city at the mouth of the St. Maurice River when, not so long ago, all he could see at the station was the English name "Three Rivers"? Can we really pretend to be a vigorous French race when we accept notices and advertisements from transport and other companies in English only with the sole exception of

Défense de fumer [No smoking] and *Défense de cracher* [No spitting], when we
tolerate English as the sole language of business with clients, when we
invariably ask for a telephone number in English or accept from our public
utility companies letters written in English only, when we consult only
English menus in our restaurants and cafés? Do you think many other nations,
proud of their origins and determined to live, would tolerate such a situation
for any length of time? [2]

It was not until the 1960's that Québec governments would do
something about it. Serious language planning began with the
establishment of the *Régie de la langue française* to improve the corpus
of the French language. Its mandate was to disseminate correct
terminology in order to alleviate the negative perception many
Québécois had of Québec French relative to standard European
French. However, subsequent pieces of legislation increasingly turned
to status planning. [3] In 1968, Bill 85 (*An Act to amend the Education
Department Act, the Superior Council of Education Act and the Education
Act*) aimed at taking "the measures necessary to ensure that persons
settling in the Province of Québec may acquire, upon arrival, a
working knowledge of the French language..." [section 1] and "to
ensure a working knowledge of the French language to every person
who attends ... an English-language institution" [section 8]. The right of
parents to choose English or French schools for their children was
maintained, but most schools would have to ensure that pupils acquire
a working knowledge of French.

Although Bill 85 did not pass, its aims were successfully restated one
year later in Bill 63 (*An Act to Promote the French Language in Québec*).
Bill 63 also gave the Régie de la langue française a new mandate that
opened the door to the far-reaching status planning that was to come.
In addition to its previous functions, the Régie would now have the
duty to advise the government on measures which might be passed to
"see to it that French is the working language in public and private
undertakings..." and to ensure the priority of the French language on
public posting. It would also have the mandate to "hear any complaint
by any employee or group of employees to the effect that his or their
right to use the French language as the working language is not
respected", and be given the corresponding powers of investigation
[section 4]. Again, freedom of choice in regard to the language of

education was respected, thus enabling immigrants to choose English schooling for their children, though they would have to acquire some knowledge of French. Bill 63 was highly controversial, for it attempted to find a middle ground between immigrants' wish to choose the language of instruction and French Canadians' desire to see them integrated into the French school system. It is worth noting that these first major debates over language were occuring in a context of unrest: riots in Saint-Léonard opposing Italians and French Canadians, the creation of the separatist Parti Québécois in 1968, the terrorist actions of the marxist-leninist *Front de Libération du Québec* (Quebec Liberation Front) and, later in 1970, Québec's military occupation under the War Measures Act. Needless to say, these events only served to exacerbate the ethnolinguistic tensions.

In 1974, Bill 22 (*Official Language Act*) brought major changes to the underlying philosophy of language legislation. French was declared the official language of Québec. But more significantly, it introduced measures to channel children of immigrants into the French school system. It stated that "[p]upils must have a sufficient knowledge of the language of instruction to receive their instruction in that language", or else they would have to receive their instruction in French [section 41]. Although exceptions were provided to allow Aboriginals and Inuits to receive instruction in their own language, and although Québec anglophones could still send their children to English schools, immigrant children who did not have a working knowledge of English would have to attend French schools. Bill 22 also took measures to make French the language of communication in the public administration, public utilities and professional bodies, as well as to guarantee private sector workers the right to communicate in French among themselves and with their superior officers. In addition, the law would now require that public signs be drawn up in French, or in both French and another language [section 35].

Bill 101 (*Charter of the French Language*) grew out of Bill 22 and of the election of the Parti Québécois in 1976. More explicit and less diluted than Bill 22, it also introduced more coercive measures. Along with the same objective of channelling children in the French school system, the law would now require all children to receive their instruction in French, except those with at least one parent whose major part of his or her elementary instruction was received *in English in Québec* [sections 72 and 73]. Thus the new law abandoned the testing measures for immigrants, which had permitted anglophone immigrants to attend English schools, and left them no choice but to attend French schools regardless of their mother tongue. It also meant that anglophone parents moving to Québec from elsewhere in Canada would likely have to send their children to a French school. Moreover, Bill 101 provided for commercial signs and posters to be exclusively in French [section 58], a provision which many found needlessly irritating. Finally, it pursued francisation programs for private enterprises which had been put into gear under Bill 22. The administration of language policy was to become structured around three new boards: the *Office de la langue française* (French Language Bureau) to deal directly with status and corpus planning; the *Conseil de la langue française* (French Language Council) to monitor the progress made and advise the government correspondingly; the *Commission de surveillance et des enquêtes* (Surveillance and Investigations Commission) to take care of violations of the law.

Because they respected the freedom of immigrants to choose the language of instruction, Bill 85 and Bill 63 met considerable resistance from nationalist circles, the teachers' union, and student associations.[4] With Bill 22 and Bill 101 however, the scope of language legislation was to become much more far-reaching since they in fact conferred language rights on the French-Canadian majority and imposed more coercive measures to ensure its effectiveness. Even though the term "right" is hardly used in Bill 22, the idea of rights pervades the spirit of the law. For example, the preamble states that "the French language is a national heritage which the body politic is in duty bound to preserve", thus empowering the National Assembly "to employ every means in its power to ensure the preeminence of that language...". Rights-discourse explicitly appears in the Charter of the French Language. Under a chapter entitled "Fundamental Language Rights", it guarantees the right of every person to communicate in French within both public and private sectors, to speak French in deliberative assembly, to carry on activities in French in the workplace, to be informed in French as consumers of goods and services, and to receive instruction in French [sections 2-6]. Its preamble states that the National Assembly "is resolved therefore to make French the language of Government and the Law, as well as the normal and everyday language of work, instruction, communication, commerce and business...". Clearly we are in the presence of the expression of the strongest language right, the right to live in one's language.

We can ask ourselves whether language legislation has proven successful in providing the French Canadians of Québec with the good of living in their own language. Should it turn out that the various interventions in the educational system, the private sector and public administration were useless, their legitimacy would understandably be questioned. If it were found that there is no rational connection between the objective of promoting the French language and the legislative means used to this end, then there might be grounds for challenging Bill 101.

In that regard, Pierre Laporte explains that surveys of public *perception* seem to show that French is gaining ground as a public language in commercial transactions and advertisement. They also show that French as a language of work is making real gains insofar as it is increasingly a condition of employment in business firms, though English was still perceived in 1980 as being more useful for promotions. For example, a 1981 survey suggested that French made less gains as a language of occupational mobility than as a language of communication. As a language of instruction, French has made important gains as a direct result of Bill 101, but also because French is increasingly perceived to be a language of status: more and more children who are eligible for English schooling are nevertheless choosing French schooling. Thus considering its low costs of implementation, it would seem that the Charter of the French Language has been efficient in securing the linguistic identity of the French-speaking Québécois. [5] It is, however, a fragile result, for English indisputably remains the dominant language in North America regardless of any gains obtained through language legislation. Moreover, the provisions that force the integration of immigrants into French schools have given rise to a new challenge: some of the previously ethnically homogeneous schools attended massively by French Canadians have now become multicultural, leading to increased racial tensions and a possible loss of traditional French-Canadian values. [6]

Can we conclude that there is a causal link between Bill 101 and the improvement of the status of French? Only tentatively, for other factors have probably contributed to improving the status of French concurrently with language legislation, namely higher levels of education among French Canadians and their increased participation in the business world. It could even be argued that some of the aims of Bill 101 address primarily a socioeconomic problem rather than a purely linguistic one, as Marc Guillotte argues about francisation programs in private enterprise. [7] More generally, some view the Quiet Revolution as the major determinant in boosting the self-esteem of French Canadians in Québec. Bill 101, it is said, came later and served as a kind of shock therapy to increase the Québécois' awareness of their linguistic situation. [8] It must also be remembered that the Quiet Revolution accelerated the secularization of French-Canadian society which had been underway since the Second World War. The Church lost much of its control over the institutions and the ideology that had served to provide Anglo-American capitalists with cheap and docile French-speaking labour. In other words, French Canadians would now have better access to the economic power that had been denied them under the corporatist alliance between the government of Maurice Duplessis, the Church, and the anglophone economic elite. The politicization of language, it can be argued, followed the taking over of power by the rising, well educated, French-Canadian middle class.

Whatever the case might be, it is clear that people *believe* there is a causal link between language legislation, the improvement of the status of the French language, and the socioeconomic gains of the French-speaking Québécois. [9] As far as the language of signs is concerned, the Supreme Court's comment in this regard deserves attention:

> Thus in the period prior to the enactment of the legislation at issue [Bill 101], the "visage linguistique" [linguistic image] of Quebec often gave the impression that English had become as significant as French. This "visage linguistique" reinforced the concern among francophones that English was gaining in importance, that the French language was threatened and that it would ultimately disappear. It strongly suggested to young and ambitious francophones that the language of success was almost exclusively English. It confirmed to anglophones that there was no great need to learn the majority

language. And it suggested to immigrants that the prudent course lay in joining the anglophone community. The aim of such provisions as ss. 58 and 69 of the Charter of the French Language was, in the words of its preamble, "to see the quality and influence of the French language assured". The threat to the French language demonstrated to the government that it should, in particular, take steps to assure that the "visage linguistique" of Quebec would reflect the predominance of the French language. The s. 1 and s. 91 materials establish that the aim of the language policy underlying the Charter of the French Language was a serious and legitimate one. They indicate the concern about the survival of the French language and the perceived need for an adequate legislative response to the problem. Moreover, they indicate a rational connection between protecting the French language and assuring that the reality of Quebec society is communicated through the "visage linguistique". [10]

The notion of a *visage linguistique* is central here, for in the words of the Government of Québec, "the linguistic image communicated by advertising is an important factor that contributes to shaping habits and behaviour which perpetuates or influence the use of a language".[11] The objective is not, as some seem to believe, to irritate the English-speaking Québécois, but rather to send the message that French, not English, is the language of the majority.

The hard question is whether Bill 101 unreasonably restricted the rights and freedoms of individuals and of other linguistic communities. The exercise of a collective language right in Québec, Laurin wrote, "does not mean that many other mother tongues cannot exist or be used in private life and in the activities of individual ethnic groups".[12] This corresponds to the universal right to use one's language in one's private sphere of activity, and finds guarantees in Bill 101 itself. For example, advertising in non-French media did not have to be in French, and public messages of a religious, political, ideological or humanitarian nature could be in any language [section 59]. Moreover, the detailed regulations which accompanied Bill 101 provided more exceptions: advertising related to any cultural or educational product or activity could be both in French and in any other language(s); ordinary citizens could post messages in any language on their private dwellings; advertising during a convention, fair, exhibition, or conference could be in any language, etc. [13]

Still, the standard objection is that some provisions of Bill 101 impinge on people's right not to be interfered with or discriminated against on the basis of language. Because the Supreme Court construed

language as being intimately linked with expression—something that
the Québec government could not disagree with—it was able to
substantiate its decision that the French-only sign provisions of Bill 101
limit freedom of expression as defined in the Canadian Charter of
Rights. Viewed this way, forbidding languages other than French on
commercial signs is an unjustifiable intrusion in someone's private
sphere of activity. As the Court argued,

> [t]he respondents seek to be free of the state imposed requirement that their
> commercial signs and advertising be in French only, and seek the freedom, *in
> the private or non-governmental realm of commercial activity*, to display signs
> and advertising in the language of their choice as well as that of French.
> Manifestly the respondents are not seeking to use the language of their choice
> in any form of direct relations with any branch of government and are not
> seeking to oblige government to provide them any services or other benefits in
> the language of their choice. In this sense the respondents are asserting a
> freedom, the freedom to express oneself in the language of one's choice in an
> area of non-governmental activity, *as opposed to a language right of the kind
> guaranteed in the Constitution.* [14] [my emphasis]

In short, the respondents were arguing that the French-only signs
provisions are a violation of their individual right against undue
interference in private language use. They were not claiming a
communal language right as members of the anglophone community,
but a negative language right as members of a liberal polity. The risk
for the Québec government was that any defence for French-only signs
was double-edged: given the centrality of language, if francophones
argue that the pervasive nature of language justifies wide-ranging
interventions in society in order to protect their language, other
linguistic groups can argue that the pervasive nature of language on the
contrary justifies protection *against* state intervention which aims at
limiting their own language.

There is another reason why some parts of Bill 101 were said to
impinge on individual language rights. Since the Québec Charter of
Human Rights and Freedoms includes language in its list of items that
ought to be protected against discrimination, the Supreme Court in
A. G. Quebec v Brown's was able to rule that the French-only signs
provisions of Bill 101 discriminate on the basis of language:

> [Section 58 of the Charter of the French Language] has the effect, however, of impinging differentially on different classes of persons according to their language of use. Francophones are permitted to use their language of use while anglophones and other non-francophones are prohibited from doing so. Does this differential effect constitute a distinction based on language within the meaning of s. 10 of the Quebec *Charter?* In this Court's opinion it does. [15]

Insofar as banning the use of additional languages is concerned, the Court felt it was unduly discriminatory.

Tensions between valid moral claims in Québec do not manifest themselves exclusively in the conflict between individual language rights and community language rights, but among community language rights themselves. Bill 101 as a strong language right coexists with other collective language rights, namely those of the Aboriginal communities. For example, Bill 101 states that "[n]othing in this Act prevents the use of an Amerindic language in providing instruction to the Amerinds, or of Inuktitut in providing instruction to the Inuit" [section 87]. It further states that "[t]he Indian reserves are not subject to this act" [section 97]. That Aboriginal and Inuit peoples have community rights is acknowledged by Laurin, who wrote that unlike immigrants "the Amerindians and the Inuit are the only ones who from a certain point of view can consider themselves as peoples separate from the totality of Québécois and in consequence insist on special treatment under the law".[16] It must be stressed that the Charter of the French Language is also to coexist with the constitutional rights of anglophones: those of section 133 of the British North America Act of 1867, which states that English may be used in Québec's National Assembly and courts; and those of the Canadian Charter of Rights, which provide the anglophone minority of Québec with English schools and services.

The coexistence between community rights, however, has not always been smooth. In *A. G. Quebec v Blaikie* [1979], the Supreme Court ruled unconstitutional the provision of Bill 101 making the French version of Québec statutes and regulations the only official ones. To this end, the Court invoked section 133 of the B. N. A. Act which, as was just mentioned, provides for the use of French and English in debates, records, and acts of the National Assembly. It had been suggested that since the Manitoba legislature in 1890 had canceled section 23 of the federal Manitoba Act, which provided for the use of

French or English in the legislature and courts of Manitoba, then the
National Assembly could do the same.[17] Indeed, section 23 of the
Manitoba Act and section 133 of the B. N. A. Act were similar and, it
could be argued, had the same purpose and therefore the same status
despite the constitutionally entrenched status of the latter. In 1979, the
Supreme Court ruled in *A. G. Manitoba v Forest* that these provisions of
Manitoba's 1890 Official Language Act were unconstitutional, just as
those of Bill 101 were found to be in *A. G. Quebec v Blaikie* that same
day.[18] The point is that the constitutionally protected community
rights found in section 133 of the B. N. A. Act overrode that particular
provision of Bill 101.

Moreover, in *Quebec Association of Protestant School Boards v A. G.
Quebec* [1984] the Supreme Court struck down the so-called "Québec
clause" in Bill 101 on the grounds that it was incompatible with section
23 of the Canadian Charter of Rights. The Québec clause restricted
Canadian citizens' access to English schools in Québec if they arrived
from other provinces. The Québec submission agreed that the Québec
clause was indeed a limit on freedom of instruction, but argued it was a
reasonable limit consistent with section 1 of the Charter, which states
that rights can be reasonably limited if there are valid reasons. In short,
it argued that a community right underlies the Québec clause: it "is
reasonable because it is the expression of a collective right of the
francophone majority—vulnerable because it is a minority in Canada
and only constitutes 2.5 per cent of the population of North
America—to assure its rightful cultural security".[19]

The above cases illustrate the tension between two community
rights: the strong language rights of French Canadians in Québec and
the language rights anglophones enjoy as members of one of the official
language communities. Enforcing full compliance of both rights leads
to a clash whose resolution seems to be determined by the
constitutionally entrenched character of the latter. But regardless of the
outcome, the distinction I wish to emphasize is that we are in the
presence of an inter-community rights conflict rather than a conflict
between community language rights and individual language rights.

Were the courts' decisions fair? We can ask ourselves if there are
counter-arguments that would question the validity of these decisions.
For instance, there is a case for saying that freedom of commercial

expression overflows the realm of private activities, a case which the appellants did not attempt to make. On this view, commercial activities have a public dimension which warrants state regulation regardless of the fact that the mode of ownership is private. There is a difference between those private language activities which are intimately self-regarding, such as talking to a friend on the street or joining a club, and those language activities that interrelate with the public realm. So there is something to be said about the need to demarcate the domain of action where one is totally free to use one's language. Here the issue refers to the difficult task of drawing the line between self-regarding and other-regarding actions. It is not unreasonable to argue that this kind of commercial activity overflows the private realm and touches upon the sensibilities of French Canadians, hence justifying some regulation.

Even if it were shown that decisions about the language of signs are a private matter protected from state intervention, there would still be a case for showing that so-called "commercial" freedom of expression is a deceiving abuse of the notion of freedom of expression, and thus that it should not receive Charter protection. We can see why the idea that putting up an English-only sign constitutes fundamental expression trivializes what freedom of expression ought to mean, namely the freedom to express one's thoughts and opinions. After all, the rationale for French-only signs had nothing to do with providing more freedom of expression for francophones, but instead aimed at creating a French *visage linguistique*. Why, then, invoke freedom of expression against it? Putting up a *commercial* sign in one's language seems unrelated to fundamental expression. No one disputes that restrictions on language use in commercial activities still have an emotional impact, especially when they are perceived as a symbolic attack on the English-speaking community of Québec, sending the message that the strength of the French-speaking community is inversely proportionate to that of the English-speaking community. So there might be good reasons for watering down Bill 101, but not because it allegedly violates fundamental freedom of expression. Even if freedom of expression was understood to include commercial advertising in the language of one's choice, we can still wonder with the Government of Québec why it should receive the same degree of protection as that afforded to the expression of religious or political ideas.

We can also question the validity of the discrimination argument, that French-only signs impinge differently on people according to their language of use. The rationale for forbidding languages other than French on commercial signs in the first place is that a plurality of languages *does* have a differential impact insofar as the English language has a stronger power of attraction than French, especially in Montreal. The submission presented by the government of Québec to the United Nations (discussed below) makes the point that the exposed position of the French language in North America precludes an equal treatment of languages that would not be able to restore the imbalance.[20] It may be a case of reverse discrimination, yet one that is justifiable in Québec's case. As for those provisions of Bill 101 being discriminatory, it is hard to see how they are any less justified than other reversed discriminations based on a recognition that the free market operates to the advantage of the powerful.

I do not want to imply that the courts were insensitive to these arguments. The Supreme Court reflected some of these concerns when it legitimized the imposition of French on all commercial signs, and said it would even support its marked predominance over additional languages. I am inclined to agree with its proposed compromise, though one could argue that the explanations given for calling some of Bill 101's restrictions unreasonable are on shaky grounds.

So really there are two kinds of interpretations. The first one is to conceive commercial expression as fundamental expression and/or as part of the private realm, and point to Bill 101's unreasonable limits and intrusions. This point of view is more or less the one the Supreme Court adopted. Adjudication would then involve balancing these rights with the promotion of the French-speaking identity through Bill 101. The second one is to understand commercial expression as not being fundamental expression nor part of the private realm, and thus not construe the conflict as one between valid moral claims. That would lead to a different kind of resolution which might have involved, for example, saying that commercial expression, though important, is not fundamental, and that commercial signs, though important to the owners, are public in the same way that automobile licence plates are.

In the midst of these debates over language rights, we often forget that the more coercive aspects of Bill 101 do not exempt French Canadians themselves. Just like any other Québec residents, they too are bound by Bill 101. So much importance do we attach to inter-community tensions that we neglect to consider how French Canadians in Québec must themselves take up the duty to promote the French language, that it is not only a matter of defending it against "outside" forces. Until they are willing to freely conform to their own rules, French Canadians must be protected against the dangers of assimilation that exist within them, against the temptation to submerge into North American society. There are therefore distinct reasons for no differently imposing on French Canadians the duties that correlate with the promotion of French as a communal good. With community membership come certain duties to respect the good of the community, especially if non-respect leads to the disruption of the community's values that are central to its identity. This justifies constraining unwilling members on the grounds that membership entails certain obligations. Some form of coercion may become even more necessary when the central communal good is one that is necessarily shared, and thus one which requires a sustained network of participants.

In other words, being a member of the French-Canadian community of Québec imposes certain obligations. On these grounds there exists another class of restrictions altogether for those who decide to take a free ride. Someone could enjoy a communal good without the burden of having the duty to contribute to its preservation. I may enjoy the language I speak as a French Canadian, and yet insist on having my children educated in English to increase their chances of upward mobility. Knowing this, my community might feel justified in forcing a duty upon me to have my children educated in French instead of my counting on the others to preserve it. I am thinking here of those French-Canadian parents who wish to send their children to English schools as long as no one else does the same. This way their own children might have better chances at upward mobility and Québec would remain French!

Liberals are not necessarily unsympathetic to coercion that prevents free riding. J. S. Mill argued that state intervention is justified in those cases where "[i]t is the interest of each to do what is good for all, but only if others will do likewise". He went on to say that coercion is necessary "because even an unanimous opinion that a certain line of conduct is for the general interest, does not always make it people's individual interest to adhere to that line of conduct".[21] Coercion is here justified on the basis that agreeing that something is a good—especially when it is claimed as a matter of right—means agreeing to the enforcement of obligations for all those who benefit from it.

Many will not be convinced by the arguments presented so far. It is, to be sure, a delicate situation when two or more linguistic communities make valid, yet sometimes incongruous, claims. Because this is what the issue is all about: a conflict of rights. But our sense of what rights are meant to secure ought to encompass more than the respect for narrowly defined language rights. Rights are also meant to secure the conditions for language communities to prosper. In Québec, the competing claims have produced two distinct areas of tension. One opposes a certain kind of language right that carries a seemingly universal authenticity in virtue of its wide recognition in liberal societies to another kind of language right that is rooted in the French-Canadian community. The other area of tension opposes the latter with the constitutional rights of the anglophone community. There is no a priori solution to these conflicts, but surely a better understanding of the nature of each claim can help us work out the inevitable collision.

A number of changes have been made to Bill 101 since 1977, all on the side of softening its impact. Two of them have already been discussed: in 1979, when the Supreme Court invalidated the provision making the French version of statutes the only official ones, and in 1984, when the Supreme Court invalidated the Québec clause that limited English Canadians' access to English schools. A most welcomed amendment to Bill 101, initiated by the National Assembly, was also promulgated in 1984. Bill 57 improved the preamble in order to give explicit recognition to the English-speaking community, distinct from that of other ethnic minorities in Québec. It also removed restrictions that were considered too stringent in their imposition of French within English institutions, for example in hiring policies and in internal communications.[22]

Following the 1988 Supreme Court ruling on the provisions of Bill 101 dealing with the language of commercial signs, the Liberal government introduced Bill 178 in order to comply with some portions of the ruling—and bypass others. A politically awkward piece of legislation, it would continue to forbid languages other than French on commercial signs outside establishments, while allowing additional languages to be posted inside, with the requirement that French be predominant. For Bill 178 to be constitutional, the government had to invoke section 33 of the Charter of Rights and Freedoms, which allows any government to vote a law notwithstanding specific Charter rights.

In 1993, Bill 101 (as amended by Bill 178) was once again put to the test, this time by a ruling of the Human Rights Committee of the United Nations. The plaintiffs put forth a case against the continued requirement of French-only signs outside commerces as decreed by Bill 178. They argued that their individual rights were still being violated despite the 1988 Supreme Court ruling, namely the right to freedom of expression and against discrimination. They also argued that the use of the "notwithstanding" clause, exempting Bill 178 from compliance with both the Canadian and Québec charters of rights, denied them any domestic remedy, hence the reason for turning to the United Nations.

The Human Rights Committee's ruling is interesting in many respects. It agreed with the plaintiffs that French-only outdoor advertising violates article 19(2) of the International covenant on civil and political rights (see chapter 6), which guarantees freedom of expression. Article 19(2), the Committee wrote, is not confined to means of political, cultural or artistic expression: "In the Committee's opinion, the commercial element in an expression taking the form of outdoor advertising cannot have the effect of removing this expression from the scope of protected freedom".[23] Not unlike the 1988 Supreme Court decision, the Committee believed that there are no rational grounds for prohibiting commercial advertising in English in order to protect the vulnerable position of French in North America. But unlike the Supreme Court, the Committee did not agree that anglophones were victims of discrimination for not being permitted to post English signs. They argued that both English- *and* French-speakers were prohibited from doing so, and therefore that there had been no violation of article 26 of the Covenant, which forbids discrimination.

The government of Québec responded with Bill 86 which amends Bill 101 by allowing languages other than French to be used in commercial advertising, so long as French is predominant. However, the government kept some room to manoeuvre by way of regulations that accompany Bill 101, and that can still determine where French-only signs will apply.

So where does this lead? To some, the picture which emerges so far is that of a language law which favors the ethnic majority to the detriment of basic universal rights to speak one's language and not be discriminated against for doing so. What is defective in this picture is that it does not treat the issue as a tension between equally valid moral claims. I have suggested that the authenticity of some of these claims may appear more obviously universal because they pertain to our membership in the liberal community, while other claims would be validated by a close examination of circumstances, namely historical ones, that recognize the worth of other communal attachments. The underlying rationale of the Charter of the French Language falls under the latter. Thus conceptualized, there are reasons for holding it as a morally valid state action and to evaluate its undesirable aspects as resulting from the clash with other equally valid claims.

Viewed this way, the Québec situation is very different from cases where a government infringes on individual language rights for reasons which have no moral grounds whatsoever. That was the case in 1918 when a federal order-in-council prohibited German-language newspapers in Canada, affecting the life of German-speaking communities, like that of Kitchener, Ontario. [24] The ban was certainly not the result of the exercise of some communal right by the English-speaking majority, but the unfortunate product of anti-German sentiment in the context of the First World War. This event illustrates a clear and unwarranted violation of the right to speak one's language within one's sphere of private activities, namely here the right to publish a private newspaper in one's language.

Unjustified infringements on individual language rights also sadly sum up much of French Canada's experience of Confederation outside Québec. Understanding the violations of the rights of French-Canadian minorities is not an easy task, since they are intermingled with the issue of separate denominational schools. Some cases of what on the surface appeared to be an opposition to a publicly funded Catholic school system were probably a circumvented way of undermining the support system of the French-Canadian community which was incidentally Roman Catholic. By the end of the nineteenth century, French Canadians saw the separate school system as a way of preserving not only the Catholic faith but also the French language. The evolution of the identity of French Canadians from being religion-based to becoming language-based seems to have had an impact on the nature of conflicts with the English majority. In the years after Confederation, being French Canadian was intimately linked with being Roman Catholic; correspondingly, attacks on the French-Canadian community would take the shape of governmental oppositions to Catholic separate schools. The official reason for restricting and prohibiting these was the need to have a uniform and centralized educational system, not an opposition to the French language per se. But when religion became less central to the identity of French Canadians, to be replaced by language, attacks on the French-Canadian community shifted to a more explicit opposition to French instruction as such. Many anglophone Roman Catholics themselves opposed instruction in French, wishing to "wipe out every vestige of bilingual teaching in the public schools of this Diocese", as one Roman Catholic Bishop once said in 1910.[25] It is therefore often difficult to isolate cases of French language rights violations from cases of denominational rights violations. With time however, the conflicts became more clearly based on language. In any case, all seems to suggest that the attacks were aimed to weaken the identity of the French-Canadian community, whether it be via an attack on their religion, or an attack on their language.

The language rights of French Canadians outside Québec have been impinged upon many times and to different degrees. There is no point in drawing a complete inventory of these violations, hence a few examples will suffice. If we look at education, their right to an educational regime suited to their religious and linguistic needs was an integral part of the spirit of the Confederal pact, though its terms remained ambiguous as far as the written constitution goes. Typically, violations of this right involved a deliberate policy of assimilation restricting or banning the study of (or in) French in schools or the more indirect dismantling of the Catholic schools—which is what New

Brunswick did in 1871 and Manitoba in 1890. Ontario's notorious Regulation 17 (1912) was designed in effect to destroy the French-Canadian community in Ontario—the largest outside Québec—by restricting French to one hour per day in all of the province's schools. Either assimilation would occur in school, or alienated French-speaking children would drop out of school and provide a docile and uneducated labour force; either way Franco-Ontarians would be kept in their place. Reactions varied, from simple non-compliance to the development of a tacit modus vivendi, but in crucial aspects French-language education was rendered impotent for decades, and the loss to the Franco-Ontarian community is incalculable. Only in 1968 did the Ontario government approve public funding of French elementary and secondary schools, and for that matter with reluctance and constant fear of an English backlash. [26] Marc Cousineau is eloquent on the effects of such a policy on Franco-Ontarians:

> My community continues to feel the effects of years of being denied secondary education in our language. Our functional illiteracy rate is double that of the anglophone community. Among a sizeable portion of our population, the rate is above 35 per cent. Only half as many Franco-Ontarians attend post-secondary institutions as do their anglophone counterparts. Not only is this a terrible waste of a community's and nation's potential, it also condemns a significant proportion of a generation to poverty, low self-esteem, and strong alienation toward society and toward those who have received the full benefits of membership in our country. [27]

It is all the more frustrating to hear advocates of an English-only Canada call for the end of "privileges" accorded to French Canadians on the grounds that their numbers are dwindling in some parts of Canada. Why they number so few is largely the result of past intolerance and oppression, a reality that is conveniently omitted in arguments against official bilingualism that narrowly focus on present-day statistics.

Today, limiting minority language educational rights for French Canadians often takes the form of a "failure of local or provincial authorities to approach the interpretation of Section 23 [of the Charter] with openness and generosity". [28] As the Commissioner of Official Languages notes, "[t]he effect in some jurisdictions was to deprive a generation of minority official language children of the type and quality of education to which they were entitled."[29] Even after the Supreme Court's ruling in *Mahé v Alberta* [1990], which broadened the Charter right of francophone minorities to French schools to include the right to manage and control their own school boards, several provincial governments have been stalling its enforcement.[30] On the issue of legislative and judicial bilingualism, most provinces do not recognize any rights for francophones, and some who did have attempted to abolish them. We have already mentioned the 1890 Manitoba Act which not only ended the official status of French in the legislature and courts, but banned its use. More recently the Supreme Court of Canada ruled in *R. v Mercure* [1988] that Alberta and Saskatchewan were bound by Section 110 of the 1891 North-West Territories Act which provides for legislative and judicial bilingualism.[31] But since these rights were not entrenched in the Constitution, both provinces immediately moved to pass legislation modifying the Act in order to abolish the rights in question.

What is important to note here is that these are not cases of inter-rights conflict. The rationale for limiting language rights outside Québec is assimilation to the English majority on grounds of cost-efficiency and/or cultural imperialism, for which there could be no valid justification. What I want to emphasize is that the situation is different outside Québec: different of course because communal rights for French Canadians are a question of survival, making their violation all the more morally reprehensible, but different also because their violation is a case of plain repression against French-Canadian minorities rather than the result of the exercise of some communal English-Canadian right.

Most of the restrictions on rights imposed by Bill 101 are justified, whereas limitations imposed on the full exercise of French Canadians' rights outside Québec are not. Some will say this statement is a flagrant double standard and is offensive to our conception of equality. That is unfortunately how the justifications for Bill 101 have often been described by its antagonists. Is it not the last straw, they say, that after all our efforts to make Canada bilingual to suit the Québécois, they should now want to implement a policy of unilingualism? To this we can answer that official bilingualism, as entrenched in the Charter of Rights, still applies to federal institutions in Québec regardless of Bill

101, so that Québec anglophones have access to services in English. As far as constitutional guarantees for bilingualism in provincial institutions are concerned, they are only found in New Brunswick and, to a lesser extent in Québec and Manitoba. It is therefore false to maintain that Québec is unilingual while the rest of Canada is bilingual, since federal bilingualism applies in Québec and since provinces do not, as a rule, guarantee bilingualism within their own provincial institutions. What Bill 101 does is give French Canadians in Québec the possibility to live in French in the same way that anglophones in the rest of Canada can live in English. Why the Québec government needs to legislate language use to that effect should be clear to all: left to the free market of languages, French will not survive long in North America. Why French Canadians in Québec have a *right* to fight market forces also rests on solid grounds.

I do not pretend that conflicts over Bill 101 are resolved by such arguments. The problem, however, is that Canadians have grown accustomed to seeing Bill 101 as an affront to their most precious rights as they remain blind to pertinent considerations that might shed new light on their moral evaluation of it. The dominant discourse on rights indeed leaves little room for the value of communal identity and its concrete expression in community rights. Any defence of Bill 101 must overcome these obstacles which, it must be emphasized, are not inherent to the Canadian federal system but rather to a version of liberal ideology. We must remember that the Supreme Court of Canada's rulings against Bill 101 *upheld* decisions that the Superior Court of Québec and the Québec Court of Appeal had previously arrived at. And we must remember that not only the Canadian Charter of Rights and Freedoms, but Québec's own Charter of Human Rights was also cited in the cases. The problem, then, is not between Ottawa and Québec, but between liberalism and community; an independent Québec would no less be faced with the difficult challenge of striking the proper balance between valid moral claims.

Notes

1. Parts of this chapter are based on my previously published article "Making Sense of Law 101 in the Age of the Charter", *Québec Studies* 17 (Fall 1993/Winter 1994).

2. Groulx, "L'Action française", 71. My translations.

3. On the various pieces of language legislation, see Daoust-Blais, "Corpus and Status Language Planning in Quebec: A Look at Linguistic Education", 217-229, and Alison d'Anglejan, "Language Planning in Quebec: An Historical Overview and Future Trends", in *Conflict and Language Planning in Quebec*, 36-45.

4. Bergeron, *Pratique de l'État au Québec*, 124.

5. Laporte, "Status Language Planning in Quebec: An Evaluation", 62-75

6. See Lachapelle et al., *The Quebec Democracy*, 348.

7. Marc Guillotte, "L'aménagement linguistique dans l'entreprise privée au Québec", *Actes du Colloque international sur l'aménagement linguistique*, 345.

8. Julien Bigras, "La langue comme pierre angulaire de l'identité québécoise", *L'oiseau-chat: roman-enquête sur l'identité québécoise*, ed. Hervé Fischer (Montréal: La Presse, 1983), 182.

9. Laporte, "Status Language Planning in Quebec: An Evaluation", 75.

10. Supreme Court of Canada, *The Attorney General of Quebec v La Chaussure Brown's Inc.*, 72-73. My translation.

11. Quoted by the Human Rights Committee of the United Nations, Forty-seventh session, 5 May 1993, 11.

12. Laurin, "Charte de la langue française", 122.

13. Office de la langue française, *Regulation respecting the language of commerce and business*, sections 8, 12, 14.

14. Supreme Court of Canada, *The Attorney General of Quebec v La Chaussure Brown's Inc.*, 41.

15. Supreme Court of Canada, *The Attorney General of Quebec v La Chaussure Brown's Inc.*, 83.

16.   Laurin, "Charte de la langue française", 122.

17.   See Claude-Armand Sheppard, *The Law of Languages in Canada*, vol. 10 of *Studies of the Royal Commission on Bilingualism and Biculturalism* (Ottawa: 1971), 103-105.

18.   Peter H. Russell, *Leading Constitutional Decisions* (Ottawa: Carleton University Press, 1982), 460-461.

19.   Quoted by Roger Gibbins, *Conflict and Unity* (Agincourt: Methuen, 1985), 63.

20.   Human Rights Committee of the United Nations, Forty-seventh session, 5 May 1993, 11.

21.   J. S. Mill, *Principles of Political Economy* (Toronto: Penguin Books, 1970), 332.

22.   On Bill 57, see Alain-G. Gagnon and Mary Beth Montcalm, *Quebec Beyond the Quiet Revolution* (Scarborough: Nelson, 1990), 187-188.

23.   Human Rights Committee of the United Nations, Forty-seventh session, 5 May 1993.

24.   This event is reported in the following sources: John English and Kenneth McLaughlin, *Kitchener: An Illustrated History* (Waterloo: Wilfrid University Press, 1983), 128; Gottlieb Leilbrandt, *Little Paradise: The Saga of the German Canadians of Waterloo County, Ontario, 1800-1975* (Kitchener: Allprint Company Limited, 1980), 158, 253; Herbert Karl Kalbfleisch, *The History of the Pioneer German Language Press of Ontario, 1835-1918* (Toronto: University of Toronto Press, 1968), 106.

25.   Bishop Fallon of London, quoted in Report of the Royal Commission on Bilingualism and Biculturalism, *Book II: Education* (Ottawa: Queen's Printer, 1968), 49.

26.   Wardhaugh, *Language and Nationhood: The Canadian Experience*, 115.

27.   Marc Cousineau, "Belonging: An Essential Element of Citizenship — A Franco-Ontarian Perspective", in *Belonging: The Meaning and Future of Canadian Citizenship*, 145.

28.   Commissioner of Official Languages, *Retrospective: From One Crisis to Another*, Annual Report 1990 (Ottawa: Minister of Supply and Services, 1991), xvi.

29. Commissioner of Official Languages, *Retrospective: From One Crisis to Another*, xvi.

30. Commissioner of Official Languages, *Retrospective: From One Crisis to Another*, xix.

31. Commissioner of Official Languages, *Retrospective: From One Crisis to Another*, xvi.

8

Citizenship and Modernity

Understood in a broad sense and in its modern form, citizenship evokes our membership in the political community and says something about the values that nourish our allegiance to it. It is a most noble trait of modern political communities that mutual respect and concern should arise out of our equal citizenship, not out of our particular identities. The creation of a public sphere where all have equal worth regardless of their differences is perhaps the most welcome heritage of the French and American Revolutions. Not surprisingly, such a rich concept is central to public debate (and to constitutional discussions) as we try to define (and entrench) not only what it means to be a member of the Canadian polity, but also what it means to be a Québécois, or a New Brunswicker, etc. Such is the federal nature of the Canadian polity that citizenship cannot reflect a single membership or undivided loyalty.

Citizenship is a remarkable achievement indeed, yet one that has had side-effects. Post-Charter political culture, for instance, has prompted a view of citizenship where basic individual rights and freedoms are allegedly the fundamental values that bind us together, against which all other values are to be gauged. The problem is not so much the real possibility that the Charter culture will weaken provincial ties to the advantage of canadianism, although this may be deplorable too. More important is how citizenship, as defined by the Charter culture, plays against communal attachments by relegating them to the private sphere or, at worst, by condemning these attachments as sources of division and difference among citizens. Note for example the following comment by Neil Bissoondath:

Heritage belongs to the individual. It seems to me possible to instruct an
individual child in his or her heritage without erecting ghetto walls by enlisting
in communal endeavour. Emphasizing the "I" and de-emphasizing the "we"
may be the only way to avoid the development of cultural chauvinism...
[W]hatever may come after multiculturalism will aim not at preserving
differences but at melding them into a new vision of Canadianness, pursuing a
Canada where inherent differences and inherent similarities blend easily and
where no one is alienated with hyphenation. A nation of cultural
hybrids—where every individual is unique, every individual distinct. And
every individual is Canadian, undiluted and undivided. [1]

For many French Canadians, malaise and despair, not pride and hope,
best describe membership in such a political community. They feel
their identity is assaulted in the public sphere itself, and therefore find
security in hyphenation. Hubert Guindon writes:

"Unhyphenated Canadianism" is a mirage based on the confusion of individual
biography with group history. All immigrants have a biographical break with
a past in which the country of origin somehow, to some degree, became
undesirable—often because of denied opportunity or political persecution; the
country of adoption, by the mere fact of receiving the immigrants, symbolizes
a land of opportunity or a refuge from oppression, both of which are good
reasons for thanksgiving. In contrast, the French and the English in Canada
are burdened with historical continuity. In both cases, the breaking with the
biographical past creates not a new citizen but a marginal one. [2]

Perhaps this explains why some immigrants have felt uncomfortable
with French Canadians' manifest refusal to "integrate" and become
Canadians like the others. For the immigrant, dropping the
hyphenation symbolizes accepting a new citizenship and celebrating a
new life in a better country; for the French Canadian, it symbolizes a
loss of identity and further alienation from citizenship. Why did the
appellation *Canadiens* give way to French Canadians, if not because
Confederation failed to respect their identity? Why did the French
Canadians of Québec then begin identifying themselves as Québécois, if
not because they saw Québec as the only place where they could be
themselves? Why do the Québécois of French origins today
increasingly designate themselves as Franco- or French-Québécois, if
not because the budding Québec citizenship does not succeed in
recognizing their identity?

Addressing this tension between membership in the political community, defined narrowly in terms of rights and duties, and communal ties and identity, is the ongoing challenge underlying citizenship. As Will Kymlicka and Wayne Norman argue, "the concept of citizenship seems to integrate the demands of justice and community membership ..., ideas of individual entitlement on the one hand and of attachment to a particular community on the other".[3] The recent tendency, it seems, has been to reduce the meaning of citizenship to our status as individual rights-bearers, evacuating the kind of cultural content that is deemed divisive, if not downright illiberal. Kymlicka and Norman write:

> These demands for "differentiated citizenship" pose a serious challenge to the prevailing conception of citizenship. Many people regard the idea of group-differentiated citizenship as a contradiction in terms. On the orthodox view, citizenship is, by definition, a matter of treating people as individuals with equal rights under the law. This is what distinguishes democratic citizenship from feudal and other premodern views that determined people's political status by their religious, ethnic, or class membership. [4]

The liberal separation between communal membership and citizenship is significant. Our private identity is linked with our existence as members of a community, while our public identity remains attached to our existence as citizens. This points to the problem that while the French language can be well-preserved in the private sphere, the equality provisions of citizenship may require assimilation within the public sphere.

The Canadian state did not succeed in recognizing the identity of French Canada within its notion of citizenship, for it spoke for too long of a single Canada with which all could identify without distinctions of race, language, culture, etc. Post-war achievements, it was believed, were sufficient to retain citizens' loyalty: national health insurance and welfare programs and, more recently, a Charter of Rights and Freedoms. But it was no secret that the discourse on the uniformity of status in the name of enfranchisement concealed the ethnolinguistic hegemony of English Canadians—not unlike Lord Durham's report had in 1840, though in more sophisticated ways. That is why Québec's aspirations have clashed with Canada's, for such institutions, however great achievements in themselves, could not replace the full recognition of French Québec. The entrenchment of duality in Canada's institutions, many Québec nationalists argue, was necessary to ensure French Canadians' continued adherence to the Confederal pact. Full duality would have allowed French Canadians to remain true to themselves within the federal framework. No doubt the imposition of the Constitution Act of 1982 despite the objections of Québec's National Assembly constitutes a major attack on duality, for the consent of Québec to a comprehensive modification of the Constitution, it seems, was no longer required. As Guindon writes:

> The compact (or dualist) theory of Confederation, the myth that so many French Canadians clung to so that they could symbolically legitimate a dignified commitment to the Canadian state, suffered an ignominious death with the patriation of the Constitution in 1982; one partner, they discovered, could force patriation without the consent of the other. [5]

The Meech Lake Accord (1987), which would have corrected the mistake of 1982 by constitutionally recognizing Québec as a distinct society, hence by entrenching duality, did not obtain the required provincial support in the face of widespread opposition in English-speaking Canada. For many Québec nationalists, such as Guy Laforest, the rejection of the Meech Lake Accord saw the dream of duality finally vanish from the collective imagination of the Québécois.[6]

The conflicts between Québec and the rest of Canada over the issue of duality reveal a deeper tension between the terms of political citizenship and the collective goals of French Québec. We saw how this tension manifests itself in actual Charter cases involving Bill 101. But it was also at the root of the opposition to the Meech Lake Accord. Standing firm on liberal grounds, opponents to the recognition of Québec as a distinct society could invoke the dangers that the clause represented to our Charter rights. The government of Québec, it was feared, would be armed with a constitutional tool to justify restrictions on individual rights in the name of the promotion of the French language. In French Québec, the clause was seen as a way of counterbalancing the sometimes untamed exercise of individual rights that puts obstacles to the promotion of the communal good. The distinct society clause, it was understood, was to work in conjunction with section 1 of the Charter of Rights, which reminds us that rights are not absolute and can sometimes be reasonably limited through judicial interpretation. In fact such a clause was considered an ingenious way of affirming indirectly the centrality of communal goods (such as the French language) by giving more latitude to those who interpret the Charter. This would have allowed courts to read into the exercise of these rights a communal content, thus accounting for language as a communal good and recognizing the moral weight of the corresponding claim.

It would be a mistake to conclude that the incapacity of the Canadian constitutional order to recognize the Québec-Canada duality reflects its incapacity to recognize the French-English duality at all. Of course it is a conclusion reached by many Québec separatists, either by their not so subtle semantic trick that transforms the whole of French Canada into Québec, or by their simple omission of one million francophones, or by their sad attempt to build a case for independence by citing the dwindling number of their compatriots who live outside the "homeland". The Charter, in spite of what Québec separatists often claim, has done much for French Canadians and Acadians who seem destined to a minority status. By guaranteeing services in French in federal and New Brunswick institutions and, more importantly, by guaranteeing the right to French language education and the right for francophones to control their own school boards, we can hardly say that the Charter accomplished nothing to recognize duality.

The problem with the Charter, it must be stressed, is not the Charter itself, but the political culture that has grown out of it. The Charter has endowed with a new liberal legitimacy the traditional refusal to recognize duality. Opponents to the recognition of Québec as a distinct society can now brandish the Charter and warn against the dangers such a recognition would pose to individual rights. Opponents to official bilingualism can now brandish the Charter and denounce the special unjustified treatment accorded to French-Canadian minorities—even if the Charter itself recognizes such "special treatment" as a matter of right. It allows, therefore, for a truncated conception of equality to take over the public conception of justice.

It is interesting that the modern Québec identity is defining itself in similar terms: a Québec whose institutions can now strengthen allegiance of all Québécois regardless of race, language or culture. What are these institutions? Hospital insurance, a pension plan, Hydro Québec, a modern educational system, a Charter of Human Rights, etc., in other words the same kinds of institutions on which the Canadian sense of nationhood was supposed to be built. They rest on the Quiet Revolution's ideals of secularization, progress and liberty, values which presuppose a conception of the individual as being author of his own life rather than being subject to transcendental forces.[7] They rest, in other words, on newly discovered liberal foundations.

It used to be said that the difference between Canada and Québec was that the Canadian state had created the Canadian nation, whereas the Québec nation had created the Québec state. This difference is now less pronounced, for the Québec state seems to be shaping a new Québec nation by using similar means as Canadian nation-building. It is hoped that out of this will emerge a new modern Québécois identity. Sometimes called *québécitude*, this identity awkwardly discards the ethnic component of the French-Canadian personality as a premodern notion unfit for inclusion in the definition of citizenship. I say awkwardly because it is a confused discourse, one which on the surface tries to officially reflect the necessities of modernity while at the same time pursuing an agenda which is manifestly rooted in a particular ethnicity.

The modern discourse, for example, suggests that the Quiet Revolution saw the Québécois identity vanquishing the French-Canadian identity, when language and culture as a pole of identification gave way to a set of modern institutions that are the stuff countries are made of. Yet at the same time it speaks of how "we" have taken control over "our" destiny on the Québec territory by asserting "our" majority status.[8] Who constitutes this majority, if not the old stock Québécois, that is, the Québécois of French-Canadian origins? If there is a "we-majority" on the Québec territory, there must be a "they-minority". Not that this discourse ignores that Québec, like all societies, will have to face the challenges raised by an increasingly heterogeneous population, not to mention those that are posed by the Aboriginal communities. But its celebration of the pluralist Québécois identity seems unable to completely abandon French Canadians defined in ethnolinguistic terms.

As Daniel Salée notes, if the notion of québécitude is officially open to the immigrant, it in fact speaks to those who feel united by a common experience, origin, culture, and sense of nationhood. Québécitude speaks, in other words, to French Canadians: it is made by them and for them.[9] In that regard, the comments of columnist Lysiane Gagnon are transparent and lucid. It has become politically incorrect, she writes, to ground the Québec independence movement in the *French-Canadian* nation, in other words, in ethnicity. Instead, contemporary nationalists speak of a territorial nationalism that confounds all ethnic origins but that stands on institutions sufficiently distinct from the rest of Canada to supposedly warrant separation. Economic and technocratic arguments for independence are heard, but not a word on culture! If these arguments for separation were sound, she writes, provinces like Ontario and British Columbia would be long gone. The reality is that Québec nationalism is rooted in French-Canadian nationalism: in language and culture, in a common history, in shared meanings and understandings. That is why there is an independence movement in Québec, and none in Ontario or British Columbia.[10]

Québec will face the challenges that Canada has been facing, and is about to make the same mistake that Canada has been making. That mistake is to present itself as a modern society with no particular ethnolinguistic bent, exhibiting a neutral state that does not represent French-Canadian interests in particular, but that aims instead at integrating all residents into a pluralistic political community. Only such a discourse can explain the claim made by some separatists that even if the Québécois were all English-speakers, there would be as strong a case for independence. And only such a discourse can explain the claim made by some supporters of Bill 101 that it does not intend to benefit the French-Canadian majority, but only aims at guaranteeing equal opportunities for all. It is a liberal discourse, one that has apparently become the prerequisite for accessing modernity.

I do not deny the important transformations that have occurred as the French-Canadian identity evolved into the Québécois identity. No doubt this shift in self-image has contributed to the creation of a full-fledged political community. For example, immigrants settling in Québec integrate into a *society* in which the ability to communicate in

French, not the primordial belonging to the French-Canadian ethnic group, defines membership in that society. Or again, the French Québécois increasingly see themselves as a majority on their territory, whereas Québec anglophones increasingly perceive themselves as a minority in Québec rather than as members of the English-Canadian majority. [11] And there is no denying that some of Québec's institutions are distinct in so far as they are derived from the distinct character of French Canadians themselves, the cooperative movement being a case in point. Yet these significant changes have left the Québec project ambiguous, which explains why they have been distorted in clumsy attempts at selling Québec independence.

The ambiguity is understandable. By warding off liberal values, French Canada was able to survive. Had French Canadians viewed themselves as choosing, autonomous, self-determined individuals, it is unlikely that there would be any French Canada left. Québec was not a province like the others in this fundamental sense. The belief in the plurality of self-chosen life plans had no place in a social doctrine that provided individuals with a moral outlook on life, a conception of the good. But Québec society needed to "catch up" with the rest of the modern world, which meant destroying the institutions and the moral horizon they had fostered along with it. French Canadians would now be liberated by becoming not unlike others. The emphasis on protecting the French language without purporting to promote a particular view of the good life would allow the Québécois to combine their need for community with their desire for liberty. It should therefore come as no surprise if contemporary nationalist ideology displaces what makes Québec different in ethnolinguistic terms to instead stress the idea of Québec as a distinct society, one that is ripe for independence. What justifies the independence project is no longer that they are not the same as others, but rather that their actions are their own. The ambiguity, then, comes from Québec embracing liberal values and adapting its official discourse to that end, but clinging to the personality that had been able to thrive in an illiberal society. Bill 101 then has to be sold within the logic of liberalism or else appear as a vestige of illiberal times.

Surely there must be a better way of articulating a public philosophy that bridges the conditions for modern citizenship with those for community and identity. It is at this juncture that the case of New Brunswick stands out. As was discussed in chapter 5, the province of New Brunswick has a substantial Acadian community, roughly one third of the total population. This is significant given the fact that the population of French *origins* is no higher than ten percent in Ontario and as low as four percent in Newfoundland. These percentages fall when we consider those who have French as a *mother tongue* (5.3% in Ontario and 0.5% in Newfoundland) and go down even further when we look at the language of *home* (3.8% and 0.4% respectively).[12] The circumstances in New Brunswick are perhaps such that any successful recognition of duality in that province would have little chance of seeing the day elsewhere, if only because of its homogeneous French and English population, which bears little resemblance to the largely multicultural character of some of the other provinces. Yet there is much to be said for what New Brunswick has achieved and for what it means for the reconfiguration of citizenship in Canada and in Québec.

In March of 1993, the Canadian Constitution was amended to recognize the equality of French and English communities in New Brunswick. The amendment adds to section 16.1 of the Charter of Rights and Freedoms, and reads as follows:

> 16.1   (1) The English linguistic community and the French linguistic community in New Brunswick have equality of status and equal rights and privileges, including the right to distinct educational institutions and such distinct cultural institutions as are necessary for the preservation and promotion of those communities.
>   (2) The role of the legislature and government of New Brunswick to preserve and promote the status, rights and privileges referred to in subsection (1) is affirmed.

It is a modified version of Bill 88, *An Act Recognizing the Equality of the Two Official Linguistic Communities in New Brunswick*, voted by the New Brunswick legislature in 1981. The movement for the creation of a separate Acadian province had been gaining ground in the late seventies, and so the government responded by proclaiming that New Brunswick was more than officially bilingual: its French and English communities were equal. In essence, section 16.1 means that Acadians have a right to develop their own institutions, and that the New

Brunswick state has the duty to adopt laws and policies and allocate public funds to that effect.

The new section is noteworthy for several reasons. First, it is unequivocally a recognition of community rights. As we saw in chapter 6, even the rights to services and education in French, which are formulated as being rights held by all individuals, can be considered community rights to the extend that they are intended for members of the French-speaking community. Unlike these Charter language rights, however, section 16.1 does not even pretend to speak of individual rights as it clearly speaks of the right of communities to promote their own character. It is the Acadian and English-speaking communities that are the right-holders, not just any individual. What it means, for example, is that the Acadian community might be justified in limiting the right of parents to choose the language of instruction for their children on the grounds that the linguistic purity of Acadian schools must be protected. The community is then given more power over the institutions that are central to the strengthening of the Acadian identity. [13] The communal nature of the clause, it is to be expected, gives more ammunition to those who were already up in arms about the idea of extending more rights to Acadians, in whatever form. They can now wrap their opposition in the language of liberal individualism and basic human rights. But even among those who are not unsympathetic to the Acadian cause, it is feared that the entrenchment of a community right undermines our Charter culture and more generally runs counter to liberal tradition. The motivation is different, but in both cases the objection is formulated as a defense of liberalism and individual rights.

Also of significance is the government of New Brunswick's new constitutional obligation to promote the respective identity of each community. Section 16.1 (2) clearly implies that the government now has the duty to preserve and promote the character of each community by providing each one with its own distinct educational and cultural institutions. This somewhat breaches the liberal notion that the state ought to be officially neutral amongst different conceptions of what the character of the community should be. The collective goals of the New Brunswick polity have acquired a constitutional status, they are recognized in the supreme law of the land. The upshot is a sense that to be a full member of New Brunswick one must be either English or French, that the clause symbolically excludes people of other origins.

Another interesting aspect of the section is its emphasis on the separateness of institutions. Rosella Melanson suggests that "Acadians are not separatist", but "[g]ood fences make good neighbors".[14] So the amendment is not more of the same; it is not about improving an anglophone dominated system to include and accommodate francophones, but about establishing a duality of homogeneous institutions in the sense that institutions be divided into French and English sections. The objective is seemingly not to promote biculturalism or bilingualism all across New Brunswick, but to allow each community to pursue its own goals by controlling its own institutions. Whether duality will be extended to most institutions or will remain limited to educational and cultural ones is unknown; still, many agree that it is a step towards full duality that will give Acadians the power to decide their own priorities. Some fear that this only serves to further accentuate the division of New Brunswick on an ethnolinguistic basis when we should aim instead at unifying the two communities by instilling a strong sense of provincehood. New Brunswick is not Belgium. The more extreme critiques speak of an apartheid bill that separates French from English and cuts the province into two. No doubt section 16.1 "divides" the province insofar as it recognizes two distinct societies within New Brunswick's political community. But the division being primarily about the creation of a security zone for Acadia, it is conducive to better relations between the two communities and consequently can only strengthen the provincial union. This is far from being divisive.

Critics of the amendment, in short, call upon a certain political culture that combines individualism, state neutrality, and uniformity. No wonder the section should be regarded as an unacceptable deviation from the Charter and the values it stands for if it is interpreted against such a background understanding of what liberal society is all about. The vision that nourishes these objections rests on a deficient liberalism, which in turn produces a flimsy citizenship. There is, as we saw, another version of liberalism, one which allows for the pursuit of community goals in the respect of basic individual rights. It ranks communality much higher in the scale of goods that are central to our well-being, and refuses to espouse the view that community is a simple aggregate of individuals whose interests happen to converge. It believes that nothing essential is lost if strict individualism is discarded from our public conception of justice, that, on the contrary, we find fulfilment in communal attachments. This liberalism, more concretely, believes that the Charter has room for the active state pursuit of communal goals, as section 16.1 indicates, for what is considered essential to Acadians' identity—their language and culture—can give rise to a right to the institutions that foster it.

Now a question may be asked, and rightly so, in regard to Acadia: is it not true that the amendment more deeply integrates Acadia into what remains a predominantly English-speaking New Brunswick, consolidates its minority status, and destroys all hope of acquiring the real power that comes with real autonomy? Does it not entrench the incompatibility of the Acadian identity and the New Brunswick identity and that of their respective projects? In a most insightful nationalist essay, Léon Thériault expressed in 1982 the fear that Bill 88 would forever fix Acadia's minority status. Not convinced that the law constituted a step towards the creation of real Acadian power on Acadian territory, he on the contrary suggested it might turn out to be a tactic to divert Acadians from real solutions.[15] Pierre Foucher likewise suggests that until Acadians exercise significant power and obtain more autonomy, such a constitutional amendment is an instrument that will remain under the control of the majority and that will respond foremost to its own needs. In other words, the constitutional recognition of equality is part of a dynamic that escapes Acadian control.[16] To these objections, it can be replied that section 16.1 nonetheless redefines citizenship in such a way that integration is no longer a euphemism for assimilation, that it recognizes two majorities within the province, and hence goes beyond pre-existing models of power and autonomy—models which might turn out to be detrimental to Acadia's future. Section 16.1, in that sense, is not Acadia's oath of allegiance to the anglophone project, but rather a constitutional tool to acadianize the public sphere in New Brunswick. The province is showing that accession to modernity need not involve the negation of identities in the name of individualism and uniformity. The conflict between Acadians' liberal commitments and their communal ties, between being New Brunswickers and being themselves, is alleviated. New Brunswick could very well become a polity where citizenship reflects "deep diversity", to borrow Charles Taylor's expression, where our profound attachments are publicly recognized and officially promoted.

When looking at the question of citizenship in New Brunswick against a liberal communitarian background, the amendment acquires an unsuspected importance. It is not simply a case of adding a right to the list of rights that the Canadian constitutional regime now and then amends. Much more than that, it is a case of rethinking the modern political community in a way that recognizes identity. As was mentioned above, the temptation to devoid citizenship of particular communal attachments is great for any polity that wishes to attain the status of a modern pluralistic society, canadianism and québécitude being cases in point. Section 16.1 shows a different avenue for New Brunswick to develop a modern personality, not by building a supposedly neutral state in the name of the equality of citizens, but by integrating into citizenship, hence into the public realm, our double respect for individual rights and for communal ties.

Should this analysis be too optimistic and the next few years confirm the deeply felt worry that the amendment is toothless and solely symbolic, New Brunswick will have denied itself the opportunity to construct the kind of citizenship that would have allowed it to remain united in dualism, however paradoxical this may sound. Duality must extend beyond the narrowly defined parameters of culture, education, health care, and justice to pervade every public institution and transform the whole administrative structure.[17] In other words, Acadia cannot settle for a parcel of power, but (short of becoming a province) should turn itself into a majority on its own territory. The right to live in French in Acadia, not unlike the right to live in French in Québec, must be affirmed.

It appears from what has been said, that the official conception of community in New Brunswick differs in kind from the one which dominates post-Charter political culture in Canada and official nationalist discourse in Québec. I must add, however, that Acadia itself is facing the challenge of defining its own political community, regardless of its status within New Brunswick, and runs into the same problem that Québec has been confronted with since the Quiet Revolution. Must the Acadian identity, *acadianité*, define itself foremost on ethnolinguistic grounds and limit membership to descendants of the Deported? Or, on the contrary, must acadianité encompass all those who simply choose to be Acadians, regardless of their language or origin? [18] Or, to complicate matters, is an Acadian anyone who resides in the Acadian half of the province, on its unofficial territory? Québec has had to displace its French-Canadian component in order to sell québécitude to those who fear a more autonomous Québec. Canada has had to discard duality in order to sell canadianism to immigrants. Likewise, building a modern and more autonomous Acadia may require abandoning ethnolinguistic conditions as the main criteria for acadianité. According to nationalist Jean-Marie Nadeau, an Acadian is anyone who defines himself foremost as such. [19] But again, it is difficult to imagine how Acadia could survive without language and ethnicity at its core and without a political project that endorses this. Thériault, for example, insists that the Acadian identity must not limit itself to a genealogical definition. Amongst all the criteria that define acadianité, the French language, not ethnicity nor a common history, is singled out as the most important one.[20] He expresses in this sense a desire to abandon the ethnic component and embrace a more pluralistic vision, albeit one that has the French language at its centre.

At the end of the day, it is the transparency of the public discourse in Acadia that will allow it to avoid the opacity of canadianism and québécitude. One of the greatest harms to the progress of public debate on these issues has indeed been the avoidance of acknowledging the ethnolinguistic nature of nationalist projects and, when there was enough courage to do so, of being castigated as promoting the premodern fusion of state and community. It is not surprising, then, to hear more and more double-talk on this subject.

That the main obstacle for French Canada lies in the public conception of justice has been overshadowed by the independence project in Québec. Many Québec nationalists believe that the final expression of modernity is political independence. For the Quiet Revolution to pursue its natural course, they say, Québec needs to acquire the tools of a sovereign state. However appealing this solution is on the surface, it neglects to consider the different responsibilities that come with full sovereignty. An independent Québec would likely face more pressures to conform to liberal values than if it remained in the federation. As a member of an overarching social union, Québec can justify some of its policies by invoking its minority status. It can pursue its communal goals, even those that involve restrictions on individual rights, since it is considered a more vulnerable community within a larger dominant society. For example, in its ruling on Bill 101, the Human Rights Committee of the United Nations rejected the idea that English-speaking Canadians could be considered a minority within Québec. The Committee consequently rejected their claim to receive protection under article 27 of the International covenant on civil and political rights, which guarantees cultural and language rights to minorities. [21] Had Québec been a sovereign state, its English-speaking minority would have been protected by article 27.

Besides, the same can be said about Acadia in New Brunswick. The present constitutional arrangements allow for citizenship in that province to embody the Acadian identity. We can imagine how a more autonomous Acadia would need to include every resident in its definition of Acadian citizenship, without any particular reference to the present Acadians as an ethnolinguistic community. Thériault, for example, includes in the definition of the present-day Acadian community all those who speak French, who share a common history, and who have the will to live together. It therefore excludes the anglophone minority in Acadia. But he adds that once Acadia achieves an official recognition of its territory, then we will have to identify French-speaking Acadians and English-speaking Acadians. In other words, anyone who lives in Acadia will be an Acadian. [22]

If on the surface we can look forward to this evolution as a positive step in defining a modern acadianité and québécitude, we can also see why French Canadians and Acadians will have a hard time articulating claims that are grounded in ethnicity. Regardless of their political status or the shape of their citizenship, they will always remain a minority in ethnolinguistic terms. If liberal citizenship is quite attractive to today's generation of Québécois and Acadians, and if it rings true to them given the currency of the discourse, tomorrow they will ask where they come from and who they are, and the liberal construct of citizenship may fall apart. It is in that sense that the entrenchment of Bill 88 constitutes a significant improvement in how we understand citizenship.

Notes

1. Neil Bissoondath, "A Question of Belonging: Multiculturalism and Citizenship", in *Belonging: The Meaning and Future of Canadian Citizenship*, 386-387.

2. Hubert Guindon, *Quebec Society: Tradition, Modernity, and Nationalism* (Toronto: University of Toronto Press, 1988), 139.

3. Kymlicka and Norman, "Return of the Citizen: A Survey of Recent Work on Citizenship Theory", 352.

4. Kymlicka and Norman, "Return of the Citizen: A Survey of Recent Work on Citizenship Theory", 370.

5. Guindon, *Quebec Society: Tradition, Modernity, and Nationalism*, 141.

6. For a comprehensive analysis of Canadian duality, see Guy Laforest, *Trudeau et la fin d'un rêve canadien* (Sillery: Septentrion, 1992).

7. See Lawrence Olivier and Guy Bédard, "Le nationalisme québécois, les Acadiens et les francophones du Canada", *Égalité* 33 (Spring 1993).

8. A case in point is Monique Simard, journalist and former union leader. See her article "La citoyenneté et le Québec", in *Belonging: The Meaning and Future of Canadian Citizenship*, 160.

9. See Daniel Salée, "La mondialisation et la construction de l'identité au Québec", in *Identité et modernité: les leçons de l'expérience québécoise*, ed. Mikaël Elbaz, Andrée Fortin and Guy Laforest (Québec: Presses de l'Université Laval, forthcoming Fall 1995). Also see his "Lament of a Nation: Multiculturalism and Identity Politics in Quebec", *Cultural Survival Quarterly* 18, no. 2-3 (Summer/Fall 1994): 89-94.

10.   Lysiane Gagnon, "Débats: les mots tabous", *La Presse* (Montreal), Saturday, 3 September 1994, sec. B, p. 3.

11.   See Langlois, "Identité nationale", 642.

12.   I borrow these numbers from Rand Dyck, *Canadian Politics* (Scarborough: Nelson, 1993), 66. The discussion of Bill 88 that follows elaborates on my previously published article "Citoyenneté et identité au Nouveau-Brunswick: la reconnaissance des communautés anglophone et francophone", *Égalité* 35 (Spring 1994).

13.   On *Société des Acadiens du Nouveau-Brunswick v Minority language School Board No. 50*, which discusses this issue, see Joseph Eliot Magnet, "Collective Rights, Cultural Autonomy and the Canadian State", *McGill Law Journal* 32 (1986): 183-184.

14.   Rosella Melanson, "Citizenship and Acadie: The Art of the Possible", in *Belonging: The Meaning and Future of Canadian Citizenship*, 133.

15.   Léon Thériault, *La question du pouvoir en Acadie* (Moncton: Éditions d'Acadie, 1982).

16.   Pierre Foucher, "Droits linguistiques en Acadie: De la dynamique des droits à celle des autonomies", in *Vers un aménagement linguistique de l'Acadie du Nouveau-Brunswick*, 67-82.

17.   For a legal interpretation of the scope of section 16.1, see Serge Rousselle's comment "La reconnaissance constitutionnelle de l'égalité des deux communautés linguistiques du Nouveau-Brunswick", *Bulletin CCDL* 1 (April 1993).

18.   See Thériault, *La question du pouvoir en Acadie*, 60-61.

19.   Jean-Marie Nadeau, *Que le tintamarre commence!* (Moncton: Les Éditions d'Acadie, 1992), 31.

20.   Thériault, *La question du pouvoir en Acadie*, 59-62.

21.   Human Rights Committee of the United Nations, Forty-seventh session, 5 May 1993, 15-16.

22.   Thériault, *La question du pouvoir en Acadie*, 61-62.

Conclusion

One of the main obstacles to French Canada's language rights is the crude version of liberalism that increasingly dominates public consciousness. Those who adhere to this kind of liberalism object to official bilingualism at the federal level because they say it violates the equality of citizens by giving preferential treatment to one group in particular. They object to New Brunswick's Bill 88 on the grounds that it divides the province along ethnolinguistic lines and elevates community rights above individual rights. They object to Québec's Bill 101 because it restricts freedom of expression and discriminates against non-francophones. Overall, they object to any language policy that departs from a view of justice based on state neutrality and on equal concern and respect. Public philosophy in English-speaking Canada has been sufficiently instilled with this kind of liberalism to preclude a constitutional reform that would truly reflect the French-English duality. Even the gains that have been made in the last thirty years are no longer secure.

Vernon Van Dyke captures well the charge against this version of liberalism when he writes that "[t]hose in a majority community can insist on individualism and the nondiscriminatory treatment of individuals, and can decry any differentiation based on race, language, or religion, knowing that this formula assures their dominance".[1] It is this very formula that assures the dominance of North American society over French Canada. French Canadians and Acadians cherish liberal values. But they are also aware that such values can be distorted and used as ammunition against the pursuit of their collective goals. For those who oppose strong language rights, that is precisely what makes liberalism attractive: to put obstacles before government actions based on political expediency. What I have been saying is that the promotion of the French language is not a matter of expediency, but a matter of justice.

Liberalism, as we have seen, need not be reduced to its crude version, and can on the contrary be consistent with our communality. Community rights, for example, may be conceived in a way that allows them to coexist along with the liberal system of individual rights. Some people, however, believe that this qualified liberalism conceals a greater danger. They may object, for instance, that it even suffers from an implicit conservatism, that in the end it endorses political projects where traditions reign over individual emancipation. In the name of French Canada's communal identity, they fear, is there not a danger that communitarian-inspired politics will not stop at the promotion of language, but will for example practice exclusion? Is there not a fine line between a defense of French Canada's language rights and the most destructive form of intolerance, that which is based on ethnicity?

There is no denying that a society should have as a goal the liberation of individuals from oppressive economic structures and social roles. A glance at history will reveal why today we value basic liberal principles, and why they sometimes ought to take precedence over settled traditions, such as the exclusion of women, the repression of individual sexual preference, the intolerance towards religious minorities, to name only a few. [2] In light of the wave of ethnic rivalries which in the form of civil wars continue to cause much grief in the world, it is not surprising that ethnicity should have become a dirty word. That we should transcend ethnic differences instead of elevating them over our common humanity leaves no doubt. [3]

However serious these concerns, they are misguided about the nature of French Canada's communal goals. The promotion of the French language does not aim at suffocating individuals under the yoke of community. Yet French Canada cannot be completely neutral before the goal to preserve a French-speaking society and the goal to abandon it in the name of purely individual pursuits. Québec governments, for example, cannot be denied the right to pursue this most valuable objective of promoting French and, to that extent, cannot but favour a certain vision of the good life. The same can be said for the government of New Brunswick which cannot be expected to remain neutral in linguistic matters and thus not endorse a citizenship with cultural content. But these government actions need not remove safeguards for basic rights nor depreciate those who do not share French Canada's vision. In other words, Québec and Acadia can remain liberal in fundamental ways and at the same time endorse policies that promote a particular good, namely the French language.[4] Should this still be judged as an unwise departure from liberal principles, then the Supreme Court itself is guilty of erring. Indeed, its ruling on the language of commercial signs sanctions Québec's pursuit of communal goals in the respect of fundamental human rights.

Besides, a case can be made that a society of atomized individuals is more likely to foster intolerance than a society of situated citizens. There is indeed a fine line between "liberating" individuals from their community and uprooting them. In its extreme form, liberal individualism invites the spirit of totalitarianism, as Robert Nisbet argued:

> It is absurd to suppose that the rhetoric of nineteenth-century individualism will offset present tendencies in the direction of the absolute political community. Alienation, frustration, the sense of aloneness—these, as we have seen, are major states of mind in Western society at the present time.

It is a state of mind which paves the way for the totalitarian project "to 'rescue' masses of atomized individuals from their intolerable individualism". He goes on to say that

> to recognize the role of privacy and the importance of autonomies of choice is to be forced to recognize also the crucial problem of the *contexts* of privacy and personal choice. For man does not, cannot live alone. His freedom is a social, not biologically derived, process.[5]

Given the importance of communal identity to a healthy society, the insinuation that Québec's dedication to promote the French language is the sign of an intolerant society, ripe for a "fascist" government should Québec become independent, rests on shaky grounds. Securing the French language is perhaps the best way to prevent a void of identity that will only lead to further social dislocation and personal alienation. To quote Charles Taylor:

> A society like Quebec cannot but be dedicated to the defense and promotion of French culture and language, even if this involves some restriction on individual freedoms. It cannot make cultural-linguistic orientation a matter of indifference. A government that could ignore this requirement would either

not be responding to the majority will, or would reflect a society so deeply
demoralized as to be close to dissolution as a viable pole of patriotic allegiance.
In either case, the prospects for liberal democracy would not be rosy. [6]

The desire to adapt liberalism to our communality does not
constitute a slippery slope towards a closed and intolerant society.
There is no incompatibility between a commitment to liberal
principles and a respect for communal ties.[7] On the contrary,
alienation and intolerance are more likely to occur in a society of
uprooted individuals who have lost their sense of identity.

The need to recognize the importance of community in our
conception of justice is also crucial to French Canada's unity. Liberal
individualism has contributed to dividing French Canada. The malaise
between French Québécois and French Canadians has its source in the
changes that have taken place in Québec since the Quiet Revolution.
Lawrence Olivier and Guy Bédard's analysis is insightful in that regard.
They suggest that the emergence of the term "Québécois" to replace the
term "French Canadian" reflects the deep causes of Québec
nationalism's disregard for French-Canadian and Acadian minorities.
Officially, the new Québécois define themselves independently of
ethnicity as they embrace the modern values of the Quiet Revolution
that to this day continue to supply the nationalist line. They are
learning to identify not with language, ethnicity, or religion, but with
progress, individualism, and consumption. However, the traditional
values of language, ethnicity, and to some extent religion, still nurture
the French-Canadian and Acadian identities outside Québec. This
reminds the Québécois that abandoning these values was the price to
pay for acceding modernity, and that they are left with an identity that
lacks substance. According to Olivier and Bédard, denying the
existence of French-Canadian and Acadian minorities is how the
Québécois repress the pre-Quiet Revolution image of themselves, an
image either rejected as an obstacle to modernity, or as a reminder of a
lost identity. [8]

That French Canada is deeply divided also stems from the stances
that Québec has taken to defend its provincial autonomy in so far as
some of these positions have worked against French Canadians living
outside Québec. For example, in 1890 the government of Manitoba
passed legislation that abolished the Roman Catholic separate school

system, hence that ended public funding for French schooling, despite the constitutional guarantees of the B. N. A. Act of 1867. Even though the central government had (at the time) the power to disallow the provincial legislation, it decided not to do so in the face of Québec's opposition to federal interference in provincial jurisdiction. A century later, the Supreme Court addressed in *Mahé v Alberta* [1990] whether the French-Canadian minority of Alberta had the right to manage its own school boards. Although the Court ruled in favour of Franco-Albertans, it is difficult to forget that the government of Québec was siding with the government of Alberta in its opposition to the extension of publicly funded French-language instruction.

Of course Québec's actions were not malicious in intent, but rather bound to the logic of the federal system and, more recently, to the logic of the Charter. Québec guards its provincial autonomy against federal incursions even if some interventions in provincial jurisdictions might improve the situation of French-Canadian and Acadian minorities. In recent years, Québec has fought Charter cases that could benefit French-speaking minorities because it knows that judicial decisions on the Charter in one province may also apply in Québec, consistently with the principle of the uniformity of rights.

Liberalism also risks transforming French Canada itself, and how French Canadians relate to their language at a deeper level. It may seem that community is at once so necessary and so natural to French Canadians that they would be immune to liberal individualism. But the metaphors of traditional society were largely rejected by French Canadians when they broke loose from "false" beliefs under the pressures of modernity. These were replaced by the more powerful and liberating narrative of individualism, which may eventually turn against them. As we saw, the French language is constitutive of the French Canadian's identity and prior to his individual choices and pursuits. With growing individualism, there is a risk that language becomes viewed as subservient to his rational, self-determined life plan. The reconfiguration of French Canada's identity, rendered necessary since the Quiet Revolution, may leave language as a commodity French Canadians own, suspended to the self-sufficient subject. Their relationship with the French language and culture may consequently become stale, if not fetishistic, with language rights becoming a variety of property rights. That, at least, is a possible scenario should their self-understandings succumb to liberal individualism.

How to counteract the effects of living in a sea of English is far from being easy, for the additional pressure of liberal individualism is at once coming from outside and from within. Thus among so many diverse obstacles to the survival of French Canada and the recognition of its rights, the crude version of liberalism is perhaps the most pernicious one. But there is no reason why we should not be able to incorporate in our public philosophy a commitment to communal goals in the respect of fundamental individual rights. Indeed, it is worth reminding ourselves that the defense of language rights in French Canada, such as the one that was discussed here, is a discourse very much rooted in the circumstances of the Canadian community. This has little to do with some alleged universal truth, but is rather a proposition whose moral weight comes from the deliberative activities of Canadians as situated citizens. It is we, in the political realm, who make the truth by moral agreement: it is *our* narrative. The problem is that since the Quiet Revolution, and more so since the Charter of Rights and Freedoms, we have changed the words to express the new moral commitments that are to become the basis of citizenship. In the process, we have failed in our deliberations about French Canada.

Notes

1.   Vernon Van Dyke, "Collective Entities and Moral Rights: Problems in Liberal-Democratic Thought", *The Journal of Politics* 44, no. 1 (February 1982): 40.

2.   See Amy Gutmann, "Communitarian Critics of Liberalism", *Philosophy and Public Affairs* 14, no. 3 (1985): 2.

3. Steven Rockefeller makes this point in his critique of Taylor's views on Québec's communitarian liberalism, in "Comment" in *Multiculturalism and 'The Politics of Recognition'*, 89.

4. See Charles Taylor, "The Politics of Recognition", 58-61.

5. Robert Nisbet, *The Quest for Community: A Study in the Ethics of Order and Freedom*, 245, 246.

6. Charles Taylor, "Cross-Purposes: The Liberal-Communitarian Debate", 182.

7. On the idea of a middle ground between liberalism and communitarianism, see Amy Gutmann, "Communitarian Critics of Liberalism", 13.

8. Lawrence and Bédard, "Le nationalisme québécois, les Acadiens et les francophones du Canada".

Bibliography

Abou, Sélim. "Éléments pour une théorie générale de l'aménagement linguistique." In *Actes du Colloque international sur l'aménagement linguistique*, edited by Lorne Laforge. Québec: Les Presses de l'Université Laval, 1987.

Anderson, Alan B. "The Survival of Ethnolinguistic Minorities: Canadian and Comparative Research." In *Language and Ethnic Relations*, edited by Howard Giles and Bernard Saint-Jacques. Oxford: Pergamon Press, 1979.

Anderson, Benedict. *Imagined Communities*. London: Verso, 1991.

Anglejan, Alison d'. "Language Planning in Quebec: An Historical Overview and Future Trends." In *Conflict and Language Planning in Québec*, edited by Richard Y. Bourhis. Philadelphia: Multilingual Matters, 1984.

Barry, Brian. "Self-Government Revisited." In *The Nature of Political Theory*, edited by David Miller and Larry Siedentop. Oxford: Clarendon Press, 1983.

Beehler, Rodger. "Autonomy and the Democratic Principle." *Canadian Journal of Philosophy* 19, no. 4 (December 1989).

Bell, Daniel. *Communitarianism and Its Critics*. Oxford: Clarendon Press, 1993.

Benn, Stanley I. "Individuality, Autonomy, and Communitity." In *Community as a Social Ideal*, edited by Eugene Kamenka. London: Edward Arnold, 1982.

Benson, Peter. "The Priority of Abstract Right, Constructivism, and the Possibility of Collective Rights in Hegel's Legal Philosophy." *The Canadian Journal of Law and Jurisprudence* 4, no. 2 (July 1991).

Bergeron, Gérard. *Pratique de l'État au Québec*. Montréal: Québec/Amérique, 1984.

Berlin, Isaiah. "The Decline of Utopian Ideas in the West." In *Unity, Plurality and Politics*, edited by J. M. Porter and Richard Vernon. London: Croom Helm, 1986.

Bernard, André. *La politique au Canada et au Québec.* Sillery: Les Presses de l'Université du Québec, 1982.

Berry, Christopher J. "Nations and Norms." *The Review of Politics* 43, no. 1 (January 1981).

Bigras, Julien. "La langue comme pierre angulaire de l'identité québécoise." In *L'oiseau-chat: roman-enquête sur l'identité québécoise,* edited by Hervé Fischer. Montréal: La Presse, 1983.

Bissoondath, Neil. "A Question of Belonging: Multiculturalism and Citizenship." In *Belonging: The Meaning and Future of Canadian Citizenship,* edited by William Kaplan. Montreal and Kingston: McGill-Queen's, 1993.

Bourassa, Henri. "The French Language and the Future of Our Race." In *French-Canadian Nationalism: An Anthology,* edited by Ramsay Cook. Toronto: Macmillan, 1969.

Bourhis, Richard. "Introduction: Language Policies in Multilingual Settings." In *Conflict and Language Planning in Québec,* edited by Richard Y. Bourhis. Philadelphia: Multilingual Matters, 1984.

Braybrooke, David. "A Public Goods Approach to the Theory of the General Will." In *Unity, Plurality and Politics,* edited by J. M. Porter and Richard Vernon. London: Croom Helm, 1986.

Brett, Nathan. "Language Laws and Collective Rights." *The Canadian Journal of Law and Jurisprudence* 4, no. 2 (July 1991).

Brown, Stuart M. "Inalienable Rights." *The Philosophical Review* 64 (1955).

Buchanan, Allen E. "Assessing the Communitarian Critique of Liberalism." *Ethics* 99 (July 1989).

Cairns, Alan C. *Disruptions: Constitutional Struggles, from the Charter to Meech Lake,* edited by Douglas E. Williams. Toronto: McClelland and Stewart, 1991.

Canada. Commissioner of Official Languages. *Retrospective: From One Crisis to Another.* Annual Report 1990. Ottawa: Minister of Supply and Services, 1991.

———. Royal Commission on Bilingualism and Biculturalism. *A Preliminary Report.* Ottawa: Queen's Printer, 1965.

———. Royal Commission on Bilingualism and Biculturalism. *Book I: The Official Languages.* Ottawa: Queen's Printer, 1967.

————. Royal Commission on Bilingualism and Biculturalism. *Book II: Education.* Ottawa: Queen's Printer, 1968.

————. Royal Commission on Bilingualism and Biculturalism. *Book IV: The Cultural Contribution of the Other Ethnic Groups.* Ottawa: Queen's Printer, 1969.

Chaika, Elaine. *Language: The Social Mirror.* Rowley: Newburry House, 1982.

Clark, David B. "The Concept of Community: A Re-Examination." *The Sociological Review* 21, no. 3, New Series (August 1973).

Clift, Dominique, and Sheila McLeod Arnopoulos. *Le fait anglais au Québec.* Montréal: Libre Expression, 1979.

Cobb, Christopher H. "Basque Language Teaching: From Clandestinity to Official Policy." *Journal of Area Studies* 11 (Spring 1985).

Connell, Tim. "Language and Legislation: The Case of Catalonia." *Journal of Area Studies* 11 (Spring 1985).

Connolly, William. "Identity and Difference in Liberalism." In *Liberalism and the Good*, edited by R. Bruce Douglas, Gerald M. Mara, and Henry S. Richardson. New York: Routledge, 1990.

Corbeil, Jean-Claude. "Commentaire de la communication de Sélim Abou: 'Éléments pour une théorie générale de l'aménagement linguistique'." In *Actes du Colloque international sur l'aménagement linguistique*, edited by Lorne Laforge. Québec: Les Presses de l'Université Laval, 1987.

Coulombe, Pierre A. "Citoyenneté et identité au Nouveau-Brunswick: la reconnaissance des communautés anglophone et francophone." *Égalité* 35 (Spring 1994).

————. "Language Rights, Individual and Communal." *Language Problems and Language Planning* 17, no. 2 (Summer 1993).

————. "Making Sense of Law 101 in the Age of the Charter." *Québec Studies* 17 (Fall 1993/Winter 1994).

————. "The End of Canadian Dualism?" *Canadian Parliamentary Review* 15, no. 4 (Winter 1992-1993)

Cousineau, Marc. "Belonging: An Essential Element of Citizenship — A Franco-Ontarian Perspective." In *Belonging: The Meaning and Future of Canadian Citizenship*, edited by William Kaplan. Montreal and Kingston: McGill-Queen's, 1993.

Cranston, Maurice. "Human Rights, Real and Supposed." In *Political Theory and the Rights of Man*, edited by D. D. Raphael. London: MacMillan, 1967.

Cunningham, Frank. "Community, Tradition, and the 6th Thesis on Feuerbach." In *Analyzing Marxism*, edited by Robert Ware and Kai Nielsen. Calgary: University of Calgary Press, 1989.

Dagger, Richard. "Rights, Boundaries, and the Bonds of Community: A Qualified Defense of Moral Parochialism." *The American Political Science Review* 79, no. 2 (June 1985).

Daoust-Blais, Denise. "Corpus and Status Language Planning in Québec: A Look at Linguistic Education." In *Progress in Language Planning*, edited by Juan Cobarrubias and Joshua A. Fishman. Berlin: Walter de Gruyter and Co., 1983.

Davies, Catherine. "The Early Formation of a Galician Nationalist Ideology: The Vital Role of the Poet." *Journal of Area Studies* 11 (Spring 1985).

Davis, Steven. "Language and Human Rights." In *Philosophers Look at Canadian Confederation*, edited by Stanley G. French. Montreal: The Canadian Philosophical Association, 1979.

Donnelly, Fred. "Geography Helps Make Quebec Distinct." *Evening Times Globe* (Saint John, NB), Tuesday, 30 August 1994, sec. A, p. 9.

Donneur, André. "La solution territoriale au problème du multilinguisme." In *Les États multilingues: problèmes et solutions*, edited by Jean-Guy Savard et Richard Vigneault. Québec: Les Presses de l'Université Laval, 1975.

Doucet, Phillippe. "Politics and the Acadians." In *The Acadians of the Maritimes*, edited by Jean Daigle. Moncton: Centre d'études acadiennes, 1982.

Dufour, Christian. *La rupture tranquille*. Montréal: Boréal, 1992.

Dworkin, Ronald. "Liberalism." In *Public and Private Morality*, edited by Stuart Hampshire. Cambridge: Cambridge University Press, 1978.

Dyck, Rand. *Canadian Politics*. Scarborough: Nelson, 1993.

Eastman, Carol M. "Language, Ethnic Identity and Change." In *Linguistic Minorities, Policies and Pluralism*, edited by John Edwards. London: Academic Press, 1984.

————. *Language Planning, an Introduction.* San Francisco: Chandler and Sharp, 1983.

Edwards, John. "Language, Diversity and Identity." In *Linguistic Minorities, Policies and Pluralism*, edited by John Edwards. London: Academic Press, 1984.

English, John, and Kenneth McLaughlin. *Kitchener: An Illustrated History.* Waterloo: Wilfrid University Press, 1983.

Espiell, Hector Gros. "The Right of Development as a Human Right." *Texas International Law Journal* 16, no. 2 (Spring 1981).

Feinberg, Joel. *Rights, Justice, and the Bounds of Liberty.* Princeton: Princeton University Press, 1980.

Finnis, John. *Natural Law and Natural Rights.* Oxford: Clarendon Press, 1980.

Fishman, Joshua A. "Conference Comments: Reflections on the Current State of Language Planning." In *Actes du Colloque international sur l'aménagement linguistique*, edited by Lorne Laforge. Québec: Les Presses de l'Université Laval, 1987.

————. *Language and Ethnicity in Minority Sociolinguistic Perspective.* Philadelphia: Multilingual Matters, 1989.

————. *The Sociology of Language.* Rowley: Newbury House Publishers, 1972.

Foucher, Pierre. "Droits linguistiques en Acadie: De la dynamique des droits à celle des autonomies." In *Vers un aménagement linguistique de l'Acadie du Nouveau-Brunswick*, edited by Catherine Philipponneau. Moncton: Centre de recherche en linguistique appliquée, 1991.

Frankena, William K. "Natural and Inalienable Rights." *The Philosophical Review* 64 (1955).

Friedrich, Carl. "The Politics of Language and Corporate Federalism." In *Les États multilingues: problèmes et solutions*, edited by Jean-Guy Savard and Richard Vigneault. Québec: Les Presses de l'Université Laval, 1975.

Gagnon, Alain-G., and Mary Beth Montcalm. *Quebec Beyond the Quiet Revolution.* Scarborough: Nelson, 1990.

Gagnon, Lysiane. "Débats: les mots tabous." *La Presse* (Montreal), Saturday, 3 September 1994, sec. B, p. 3.

Gardner, Peter. "Liberty and Compulsory Education." In *Of Liberty*, edited by A. Phillips Griffiths. Cambridge: Cambridge University Press, 1983.

Garet, Ronald R. "Communality and Existence: The Rights of Groups." *Southern California Law Review* 56, no. 5 (July 1983).

Gendron, Jean-Denis. "L'autonomie linguistique dans le cadre de l'aménagement linguistique du Nouveau-Brunswick." In *Vers un aménagement linguistique de l'Acadie du Nouveau-Brunswick*, edited by Catherine Philipponneau. Moncton: Centre de recherche en linguistique appliquée, 1991

George, Robert P. "The Unorthodox Liberalism of Joseph Raz." *The Review of Politics* 53, no. 4 (Fall 1991).

Gewirth, Alan. "The Epistemology of Human Rights." In *Human Rights*, edited by Ellen Frankel Paul, Jeffrey Paul, and Fred D. Miller. Oxford: Basil Blackwell, 1984.

Ghils, Paul. *Language and Thought*. New York: Vantage Press, 1980.

Gibbins, Roger. *Conflict and Unity*. Agincourt: Methuen, 1985.

Gingras, François-Pierre, and Neil Nevitte. "The Evolution of Quebec Nationalism." In *Quebec: State and Society*, edited by Alain-G. Gagnon. Agincourt: Methuen, 1984.

Green, Leslie. "Two Views of Collective Rights." *The Canadian Journal of Law and Jurisprudence* 4, no. 2 (July 1991).

Groulx, Lionel. "L'Action française." In *Abbé Groulx: Variations on a Nationalist Theme*, edited by Susan Mann Trofimenkoff. Vancouver: Copp Clark Publishing, 1973.

————. "Why We Are Divided." In *Voices From Quebec: An Anthology of Translations*, edited by Philip Stratford and Michael Thomas. Toronto: Van Nostrand Reinhold, 1977.

Guillotte, Marc. "L'aménagement linguistique dans l'entreprise privée au Québec." In *Actes du Colloque international sur l'aménagement liguistique*, edited by Lorne Laforge. Québec: Les Presses de l'Université Laval, 1987.

Guindon, Hubert. *Quebec Society: Tradition, Modernity, and Nationalism*. Toronto: University of Toronto Press, 1988.

Gutmann, Amy. "Children, Paternalism, and Education." *Philosophy and Public Affairs* 9, no. 4 (1980).

————. "Communitarian Critics of Liberalism." *Philosophy and Public Affairs* 14, no. 3 (1985).

Hanen, Marsha. "Taking Language Rights Seriously." In *Philosophers Look at Canadian Confederation*, edited by Stanley G. French. Montreal: The Canadian Philosophical Association, 1979.

————. "Workshop III: Report." In *Philosophers Look at Canadian Confederation*, edited by Stanley G. French. Montreal: The Canadian Philosophical Association, 1979.

Hart, H. L. A. "Are There Any Natural Rights?" In *Theories of Rights*, edited by Jeremy Waldron. Oxford: Oxford University Press, 1984.

Hartney, Michael. "Some Confusions Concerning Collective Rights." *The Canadian Journal of Law and Jurisprudence* 4, no. 2 (July 1991).

Henripin, Jacques. "Réponses aux questions posées par la Commission sur l'avenir politique et constitutionnel du Québec." In *Commission sur l'avenir politique et constitutionnel du Québec*, Document de travail numéro 4. Québec: Bibliothèque nationale du Québec, 1991.

Herzog, Don. "Up Toward Liberalism." *Dissent* 36 (Summer 1989).

Hill, Jane H. "Language, Culture, and World View." In *Language: The Socio-cultural Context*. Vol. 4 of *Linguistics: The Cambridge Survey*, edited by Frederick J. Newmeyer. Cambridge: Cambridge University Press, 1988).

Hirsch, H. N. "The Threnody of Liberalism: Constitutional Liberty and the Renewal of Community." *Political Theory* 14, no. 3 (August 1986).

Hubin, Clayton D. "Justice and Future Generations." *Philosophy and Public Affairs* 6, no. 1 (1976).

Humana, Charles, ed. *World Human Rights Guide*. Oxford: Oxford University Press, 1992.

Jacobs, Lesley. "Bridging the Gap Between Individual and Collective Rights With the Idea of Integrity." *The Canadian Journal of Law and Jurisprudence* 4, no. 2 (July 1991).

Kalbfleisch, Herbert Karl. *The History of the Pioneer German Language Press of Ontario, 1835-1918*. Toronto: University of Toronto Press, 1968.

Karmis, Dimitrios. "Cultures autochtones et libéralisme au Canada: les vertus médiatrices du communautarisme libéral de Charles Taylor." *Revue canadienne de science politique* 26, no. 1 (March 1993).

Keat, Russell. "Individualism and Community in Socialist Thought." In vol. 4 of *Issues in Marxist Philosophy*, edited by John Mepham and David-Hillel Ruben. Sussex: Harvester Press, 1979.

Keating, Michael. *State and Regionalism: Territorial Politics and the European State*. London: Harvester Wheatsheaf, 1988.

Kettle-Williams, Jay. "On Bilingualism." *Journal of Area Studies* 11 (Spring 1985).

Khleif, Bud B. "Insiders, Outsiders, and Renegades: Towards a Classification of Ethnolinguistic Labels." In *Language and Ethnic Relations*, edited by Howard Giles and Bernard Saint-Jacques. Oxford: Pergamon Press, 1979.

Knopff, Rainer. "Democracy vs. Liberal Democracy: The Nationalist Conundrum." *The Dalhousie Review* 58, no. 4 (Winter 1978-79).

Kymlicka, Will. "Individual and Community Rights." In *Group Rights*, edited by Judith Baker. Toronto: University of Toronto Press, 1994.

———. "Liberalism and Communitarians." *Canadian Journal of Philosophy* 18, no. 2 (June 1988).

———. *Liberalism, Community, and Culture*. Oxford: Clarendon Press, 1989.

———. and Wayne Norman. "Return of the Citizen: A Survey of Recent Work on Citizenship Theory." *Ethics* 104 (January 1994).

Lachapelle, Guy, et al. *The Quebec Democracy: Structures, Processes and Policies*. Toronto: McGraw-Hill Ryerson, 1993.

Laforest, Guy. *Trudeau et la fin d'un rêve canadien*. Sillery: Septentrion, 1992.

Langlois, Simon. *La société québécoise en tendances: 1960-1990*. Québec: Institut québécois de recherche sur la culture, 1990.

Laponce, Jean. *Langue et territoire*. Québec: Les Presses de l'Université Laval, 1984.

Laporte, Pierre. "Status Language Planning in Québec: An Evaluation." In *Conflict and Language Planning in Québec*, edited by Richard Y. Bourhis. Philadelphia: Multilingual Matters, 1984.

Larmore, Charles. "Michael J. Sandel: Liberalism and the Limits of Justice." *The Journal of Philosophy* 81, no. 6 (1984).

LaSelva, Samuel V. "Does the Canadian Charter of Rights and Freedoms Rest on a Mistake?" *The Windsor Yearbook of Access to Justice* 8 (1988).

Laurin, Camille. "Charte de la langue française." *Revue canadienne de sociologie et d'anthropologie* 15, no. 2 (1978).

Leclerc, Jacques. *Langue et société*. Laval: Mondia, 1986.

Leilbrandt, Gottlieb. *Little Paradise: The Saga of the German Canadians of Waterloo County, Ontario, 1800-1975*. Kitchener: Allprint Company Limited, 1980.

Lenihan, Donald. "Liberalism and the Problem of Cultural Membership: A Critical Study of Kymlicka." *The Canadian Journal of Law and Jurisprudence* 4, no. 2 (July 1991).

Lévesque, René. *An Option for Quebec*. Toronto: McClelland and Stewart Limited, 1968.

Lustgarten, L. S. "Liberty in a Culturally Plural Society." In *Of Liberty*, edited by A. Phillips Griffiths. Cambridge: Cambridge University Press, 1983.

Lynd, Staughton. "Communal Rights." *Texas Law Review* 62, no. 8 (May 1984).

MacCallum, Gerald C. "Negative and Positive Freedom." *The Philosophical Review* 76 (1967).

MacCormick, D. Neil. "Against Moral Disestablishment." In *Legal Right and Social Democracy*, edited by Neal MacCormick. Oxford: Clarendon Press, 1982.

———. "Rights in Legislation." In *Law, Morality and Society*, edited by P. M. S. Hacker and Joseph Raz. Oxford: Clarendon Press, 1977.

MacIntyre, Alasdair. "The Virtues, the Unity of a Human Life and the Concept of a Tradition." In *Liberalism and Its Critics*, edited by Michael Sandel. Oxford: Basil Blackwell, 1984.

MacMillan, Michael C. "Henri Bourassa on the Defence of Language Rights." *Dalhousie Review* 62, no. 3 (Autumn 1982).

———. "Language Rights, Human Rights and Bill 101." *Queen's Quarterly* 90, no. 2 (Summer 1983).

Magnet, Joseph Eliot. "Collective Rights, Cultural Autonomy and the Canadian State." *McGill Law Journal* 32 (1986-87).

Marie, Jean-Bernard. "Relations Between Peoples' Rights and Human Rights: Semantic and Methodological Distinctions." *Human Rights Law Journal* 7 (1986).

McDonald, Michael. "Should Communities Have Rights? Reflections on Liberal Individualism." *The Canadian Journal of Law and Jurisprudence* 4, no. 2 (July 1991).

———. "The Rights of People and the Rights of a People." In *Philosophers Look at Canadian Confederation*, edited by Stanley G. French. Montreal: The Canadian Philosophical Association, 1979.

McDonald, Virginia. "A Liberal Democratic Response to the Canadian Crisis." In *Philosophers Look at Canadian Confederation*, edited by Stanley G. French. Montreal: The Canadian Philosophical Association, 1979.

McRae, Kenneth D. "Bilingual Language Districts in Finland and Canada: Adventures in the Transplanting of an Institution." *Canadian Public Policy* 4, no. 3 (Summer 1978).

McRoberts, Kenneth. "Making Canada Bilingual: Illusions and Delusions of Federal Language Policy." In *Federalism and Political Community: Essays in Honour of Donald Smiley*, edited by David P. Shugarman and Reg Whitaker. Peterborough: Broadview Press, 1989.

———. *Quebec: Social Change and Political Crisis*. Toronto: McClelland and Stewart, 1988.

Melanson, Rosella. "Citizenship and Acadie: The Art of the Possible." In *Belonging: The Meaning and Future of Canadian Citizenship*, edited by William Kaplan. Montreal and Kingston: McGill-Queen's, 1993.

Mill, John Stuart. *Principles of Political Economy*. Toronto: Penguin Books, 1970.

———. *Utilitarianism*. Toronto: Penguin Books, 1987.

Minaudo, Vito-S. "De la noyade dans la molasse." In *L'oiseau-chat: roman-enquête sur l'identité québécoise*, edited by Hervé Fischer. Montréal: La Presse, 1983.

Moore, Margaret. "Liberalism and the Ideal of the Good Life." *The Review of Politics* 53, no. 4 (Fall 1991).

Morton, Desmond. "Divided Loyalties? Divided Country?" In *Belonging: The Meaning and Future of Canadian Citizenship*, edited by William Kaplan. Montreal and Kingston: McGill-Queen's University Press, 1993.

Morton, Frederick L. "Group Rights Versus Individual Rights in the Charter: The Special Cases of Natives and the Quebecois." In *Minorities and the Canadian State*, edited by Neil Nevitte and Allan Kornberg. Oakeville: Mosaic Press, 1985.

Nadeau, Jean-Marie. *Que le tintamarre commence!* Moncton: Les Éditions d'Acadie, 1992.

Narveson, Jan. "Collective Rights?" *The Canadian Journal of Law and Jurisprudence* 4, no. 2 (July 1991).

New Brunswick. Task force on official languages. *Towards Equality of the Official Languages in New Brunswick* (March 1982).

Nisbet, Robert A. *The Quest for Community: A Study in the Ethics of Order and Freedom*. New York: Oxford University Press, 1953.

Oakeshott, Michael. "Political Education." In his *Rationalism in Politics*. New York: Basic Books, 1962.

Okin, Susan Moller. "Justice and Gender." *Philosophy and Public Affairs* 16, no. 1 (Winter 1987).

Olivier, Lawrence, and Guy Bédard. "Le nationalisme québécois, les Acadiens et les francophones du Canada". *Égalité* 33 (Spring 1993).

Pâquet, Mgr L. -A. "A Sermon on the Vocation of the French Race in America." In *French-Canadian Nationalism: An Anthology*, edited by Ramsay Cook. Toronto: Macmillan, 1969.

Pernthaler, Peter. "Modes d'action juridique dans le domaine linguistique." *Minorités linguistiques et interventions: essai de typologie*. Québec: Les Presses de l'Université Laval, 1978.

Pestieau, Joseph. "Minority Rights: Caught Between Individual Rights and Peoples' Rights." *The Canadian Journal of Law and Jurisprudence* 4, no. 2 (July 1991).

Philipponneau, Catherine. "Politique et aménagement linguistiques au Nouveau-Brunswick: Pour de nouvelles stratégies d'intervention." In *Vers un aménagement linguistique de l'Acadie du Nouveau-Brunswick*, edited by Catherine Philipponneau. Moncton: Centre de recherche en linguistique appliquée, 1991.

Plant, Raymond. "Community: Concept, Conception, and Ideology." *Politics and Society* 8, no. 1 (1978).

Québec. National Assembly. *An Act to Amend the Education Department Act, the Superior Council of Education Act and the Education Act.* Bill 85 (1968).

———. National Assembly. *An Act to Promote the French Language in Québec.* Bill 63 (1969).

———. National Assembly. *Charter of the French Language.* Bill 101 (1984).

———. National Assembly. *Official Language Act.* Bill 22 (1974).

Rawls, John. *A Theory of Justice.* Cambridge, Mass.: The Belknap Press of Harvard University Press, 1971.

———. "Justice as Fairness: Political not Metaphysical." *Philosophy and Public Affairs* 14, no. 3 (1985).

Raz, Joseph. "Rights-based Morality." In *Theories of Rights*, edited by Jeremy Waldron. Oxford: Oxford University Press, 1984.

———. *The Morality of Freedom.* Oxford: Clarendon Press, 1986.

Regan, Tom. *The Case For Animal Rights.* Berkely: The University of California Press, 1983.

Ridler, Neil B., and Suzanne Pons-Ridler, "An Economic Analysis of Canadian Language Policies: A Model and Its Implementation." *Language Problems and Language Planning* 10 (1986).

———. "The Territorial Concept of Official Bilingualism; A Cheaper Alternative for Canada?" *Language Sciences* 11 (1989).

Rockefeller, Steven C. "Comment." In *Multiculturalism and 'The Politics of Recognition'*, edited by Amy Gutmann. Princeton: Princeton University Press, 1993.

Ross, Jeffrey A. "Language and the Mobilization of Ethnic Identity." In *Language and Ethnic Relations*, edited by Howard Giles and Bernard Saint-Jacques. Oxford: Pergamon Press, 1979.

Ross, William David. *The Right and the Good.* Oxford: Clarendon Press, 1930.

Rousselle, Serge. "La reconnaissane constitutionnelle de l'égalité des deux communautés linguistiques du Nouveau-Brunswick." *Bulletin CCDL* 1 (April 1993).

Roy, Fernande. *Progrès, harmonie, liberté: le libéralisme des milieux d'affaires francophones à Montréal au tournant du siècle.* Montréal: Boréal, 1988.

Roy, Muriel K. "Settlement and Population Growth in Acadia." In *The Acadians of the Maritimes*, edited by Jean Daigle. Moncton: Centre d'études acadiennes, 1982.

Runte, Roseann. "The Write Stuff." *Language and Society* 44 (Fall 1993).

Russell, Peter H. *Leading Constitutional Decisions*. Ottawa: Carleton University Press, 1982.

Salée, Daniel. "La mondialisation et la construction de l'identité au Québec." In *Identité et modernité: les leçons de l'expérience québécoise*, edited by Mikaël Elbaz, Andrée Fortin and Guy Laforest. Québec: Presses de l'Université Laval, forthcoming Fall 1995.

―――. "Lament of a Nation: Multiculturalism and Identity Politics in Quebec." *Cultural Survival Quarterly* 18, no. 2-3 (Summer/Fall 1994).

Sandel, Michael. "Introduction." In *Liberalism and its Critics*, edited by Michael Sandel. Oxford: Basil Blackwell, 1984.

―――. "Justice and the Good." In *Liberalism and its Critics*, edited by Michael Sandel. Oxford: Basil Blackwell, 1984.

―――. "The Procedural Republic and the Unencumbered Self." *Political Theory* 12, no. 1 (February 1984).

Saville-Troike, Muriel. *The Ethnography of Communication*. Oxford: Basil Blackwell, 1989.

Schmitz, Kenneth L. "Is Liberalism Good Enough?" In *Liberalism and the Good*, edited by R. Bruce Gouglas, Gerald M. Mara, and Henry S. Richardson. New York: Routledge, 1990.

Sheppard, Claude-Armand. *The Law of Languages in Canada*, in vol. 10 of *Studies of the Royal Commission on Bilingualism and Biculturalism*. Ottawa: Queen's Printer, 1971.

Simard, Monique. "La citoyenneté et le Québec." In *Belonging: The Meaning and Future of Canadian Citizenship*, edited by William Kaplan. Montreal and Kingston: McGill-Queen's, 1993.

Smith, Steven B. *Hegel's Critique of Liberalism*. Chicago: University of Chicago Press, 1989.

Snow, Gérard. "Quelles structures d'aménagement linguistique pour l'Acadie du Nouveau-Brunswick: bilinguisme, dualité, régionalisation?" In *Vers un aménagement linguistique de l'Acadie du Nouveau-Brunswick*, edited by Catherine Philipponneau. Moncton: Centre de recherche en linguistique appliquée, 1991.

Stewart, Edward C. "Talking Culture: Language in the Function of Communication." In *The First Delaware Symposium on Language Studies*, edited by Robert J. DiPietro et al. Newark: University of Delaware Press, 1983.

Supreme Court of Canada. *Allan Singer v The Attorney General of Québec* (December 1988).

———. *The Attorney General of Quebec v Blaikie* (1979).

———. *The Attorney General of Quebec v La Chaussure Brown's Inc.* (December 1988).

———. *Quebec Association of Protestant School Boards v The Attorney General of Quebec* (1984).

Sypnowich, Christine. "Rights, Community and the Charter." *British Journal of Canadian Studies* 6, no. 1 (1991).

Taylor, Charles. "Alternative Futures: Legitimacy, Identity and Alienation in Late Twentieth Century Canada." In *Constitutionalism, Citizenship and Society in Canada*, edited by Alan Cairns and Cynthia Williams. Toronto: University of Toronto Press, 1985.

———. "Atomism." In his *Philosophy and the Human Sciences*. Cambridge: Cambridge University Press, 1985.

———. "Cross-Purposes: The Liberal-Communitarian Debate." In *Liberalism and the Moral Mind*, edited by Nancy L. Rosenblum. Cambridge, Mass.: Harvard University Press, 1989.

———. *The Malaise of Modernity*. Concord, Ont.: Anansi, 1991.

———. "The Politics of Recognition." In *Multiculturalism and 'The Politics of Recognition'*, edited by Amy Gutmann. Princeton: Princeton University Press, 1993.

———. "Why Do Nations Have To Become States?" In *Philosophers Look At Canadian Confederation*, edited by Stanley G. French. Montreal: The Canadian Philosophical Association, 1979.

Taylor, Donald M., and Howard Giles. "At the Crossroads of Research into Language and Ethnic Relations." In *Language and Ethnic Relations*, edited by Howard Giles and Bernard Saint-Jacques. Oxford: Pergamon Press, 1979.

——— et al. "Dimensions of Ethnic Identity: An Example From Quebec." *The Journal of Social Psychology* 89 (1973).

Thériault, Léon. "Acadia, 1763-1978: An Historical Synthesis." In *The Acadians of the Maritimes*, edited by Jean Daigle. Moncton: Centre d'études acadiennes, 1982.

―――. *La question du pouvoir en Acadie*. Moncton: Éditions d'Acadie, 1982.

Tremblay, Rodrigue. "Le statut politique et constitutionnel du Québec." In *Commission sur l'avenir politique et constitutionnel du Québec*, Document de travail numéro 4. Québec: Bibliothèque nationale du Québec, 1991.

Van Dyke, Vernon. "Collective Entities and Moral Rights: Problems in Liberal-Democratic Thought." *Journal of Politics* 44, no. 1 (February 1982).

―――. "Justice as Fairness: For Groups?" *The American Political Science Review* 69, no. 2 (June 1975).

―――. "The Individual, the State, and Ethnic Communities in Political Theory." *World Politics* 29 (April 1977).

Vernon, Richard. "Moral Pluralism and the Liberal Mind." In *Unity, Plurality and Politics*, edited by J.M. Porter and Richard Vernon. London: Croom Helm, 1986.

Viletta, Rudolf. *Minorités linguistiques et interventions: essai de typologie*. Québec: Les Presses de l'Université Laval, 1978.

Waldron, Jeremy. *Nonsense Upon Stilts*. London: Methuen, 1987.

―――. "Rights, Public Choice and Communal Goods." In *Legal Theory Workshop Series*. Toronto: University of Toronto Press, 1986.

Wallach, John R. "Liberals, Communitarians, and the Tasks of Political Theory." *Political Theory* 15, no. 4 (November 1987).

Wardhaugh, Ronald. *Language and Nationhood: The Canadian Experience*. Vancouver: New Star Books, 1983.

―――. *Languages in Competition*. Oxford: Basil Blackwell, 1987.

―――. *The Contexts of Language*. Rowley: Newburry, 1976.

Webber, Jeremy. *Reimagining Canada: Language, Culture, Community, and the Canadian Constitution*. Kingston and Montreal: McGill-Queen's University Press, 1994.

Wolff, Robert Paul. *The Poverty of Liberalism*. Boston: Beacon Press, 1968.

Wringe, Colin A. *Children's Rights: A Philosophical Study*. London: Routledge and Kegan Paul, 1981.

Zachariev, Z. "Planification linguistique à l'école dans les pays multilingues." In *Language in Public Life*, edited by James E. Alatis and G. Richard Tucker. Washington: Georgetown University Press, 1979.

Index